DEVELOPING OBJECT CONCEPTS IN INFANCY: AN ASSOCIATIVE LEARNING PERSPECTIVE

David H. Rakison and Gary Lupyan

WITH COMMENTARY BY
Lisa M. Oakes
Arlene S. Walker-Andrews

D1677741

W. Andrew Collins
Series Editor

MONOGRAPHS OF THE SOCIETY FOR RESEARCH IN CHILD DEVELOPMENT

Serial No. 289, Vol. 73, No. 1, 2008

WILEY-BLACKWELL   *Boston, Massachusetts   Oxford, United Kingdom*

Suniya Luthar
Columbia University

Peter Marshall
Temple University

Robert McCall
University of Pittsburgh

Constance Milbrath
University of California,
San Francisco

Lou Moses
University of Oregon

Ulrich Mueller
University of Victoria, Victoria, Canada

Larry Nucci
University of Illinois at Chicago

Sue Parker
Sonoma University

Gregory S. Petit
Auburn University

Glenn I. Roisman
University of Illinois

Paul Quinn
University of Delaware

Karen Saywitz
Harbor UCLA Medical School

Bryan Sokol
Simon Fraser University

Elizabeth Vandewater
University of Texas,
Austin

Manfred Van Dulmen
Kent State University

David Wolfe
Center for Addiction & Mental Health
London,
Ontario, CA

Hongling Xie
Temple University

DEVELOPING OBJECT CONCEPTS IN INFANCY: AN ASSOCIATIVE LEARNING PERSPECTIVE

CONTENTS

COMMENTARY

ABSTRACT

We present a domain-general framework called *constrained attentional associative learning* to provide a developmental account for how and when infants form concepts for animates and inanimates that encapsulate not only their surface appearance but also their movement characteristics. Six simulations with the same general-purpose architecture implement the features of the theory to model infant behavior in learning about objects' motion trajectory, their causal role, their onset of motion, and the initial mapping between a label and a moving object. Behavioral experiments with infants tested novel hypotheses generated by the model, showing that verbal labels initially may be associated with specific features rather than overall shape. Implications of the framework and model are discussed in relation to the mechanisms of early learning, the development of the animate–inanimate distinction, and the nature of development in the first years of life.

I. INTRODUCTION

Of all the cognitive achievements in infancy and early childhood, perhaps none is as significant and challenging as the development of a concept of animacy. This broad representational demarcation between animates (i.e., people, animals, and insects) and inanimates (e.g., vehicles, furniture, plants, and tools) allows the developing child appropriately to distinguish, categorize, and make inductive inferences about the varied and complex things they encounter in the world. Thus, it is at the core or foundation of cognitive development in the first years of life and beyond. Yet the properties that differentiate animates and inanimates are multifaceted, and developing comprehensive representations that incorporate all of them is not a trivial task. Adult-like concepts of animates and inanimates involve not only the surface properties typically possessed by each class (e.g., eyes for animates) but also their internal properties (e.g., whether they possess a heart or an engine), and potential psychological states (e.g., whether their actions are goal-directed).

Although knowledge of these properties is unquestionably fundamental for a full understanding of the animate–inanimate distinction, a number of prominent theoretical frameworks propose that the first step along this road involves learning about the motion properties of things (e.g., Gelman, 1990; Leslie, 1995; Mandler, 1992; Premack, 1990; Rakison & Poulin-Dubois, 2001). Animate entities and inanimate objects differ markedly in their movements and their roles in motion-related events. Animals, people, and insects are characteristically agents of causal actions, tend to move without external cause, and travel nonlinearly though their environment. Inanimates, in contrast, are commonly the recipients of a causal action, require external physical force to move, and travel along linear trajectories when caused to move. Moreover, because motion-related information is available in the perceptual input (albeit intermittently), it is more easily accessible to infants than other animacy-related properties such as psychological states or biological characteristics. On occasion motion properties can be misleading because it is possible for animates to display motions typical of inanimates and vice versa (Gelman, Durgin, & Kaufman, 1995); for example, animates can be recipients of an action, and inanimates can move on nonlinear paths. Yet for the most part objects and entities in the world exhibit specific movements and play specific roles in motion events. This makes motion properties a strong candidate to be represented first as infants start to learn about the features and properties of things beyond static surface features.

In this monograph, we present a theoretical framework, simulations, and experiments that explain how infants may learn about the motion properties of object and entities in the world. In contrast to a number of previous theoretical formulations (e.g., Baillargeon, 2001; Gelman, 1990; Leslie, 1995; Mandler, 1992; Premack, 1990; Spelke, 1994), the core of this theoretical model is that the principal mechanism for object concept development is associative learning. We propose that this form of general learning mechanism, in conjunction with information-processing advances and a small number of basic inherent and emergent attention biases, is sufficient to account for the early emergence of representations for animates and inanimates. The simulations and experiments reported here, as well as those we have previously derived (e.g., Rakison, 2004, 2005a, 2006), provide only a *sufficiency account* for early concept development; that is, they do not show that associative learning is the only way in which infants can learn about motion properties of things in the world. At the same time, however, the results show how general associative processes can lead to representations that include motion properties for different object kinds across a range of different motions typical of animates (e.g., animals and people) and inanimates (e.g., tools, plants, and furniture). Note that a discussion of animates and inanimates in relation to the concepts possessed by infants does not mean that infants appreciate animacy or inanimacy in an adult sense. Instead, the terms "animate" and "inanimate" are used throughout to refer to phenomena that we, as adults, regard as falling into one of these two broad categories. The aim of this monograph is to provide a theoretical framework that accounts for how infants develop knowledge of the static and dynamic features of things in the world, knowledge that will ultimately be at the core of concepts for animates and inanimates later in life.

THE PROBLEM SPACE

How Things Look: Static Cues

There is now considerable evidence that infants' earliest representations for animals, vehicles, plants, tools, people, and other animates and inanimates are grounded in static perceptual, or surface, features (see, e.g.,

Quinn & Eimas, 1997; Younger & Cohen, 1986). We use the terms *static cues* and *static features* throughout this monograph to refer to those aspects of objects that can be extracted from a single frame; this includes features such as shape, parts, structure, color, and texture. Evidence that infants' early representations are based on such cues includes work showing that infants as young as 3 months of age within the familiarization paradigm can form categorical representations of pictures for dogs that exclude cats (Quinn, Eimas, & Rosenkrantz, 1993) and for pictures of mammals that exclude birds, fish, and furniture (Bchl-Chadha, 1996). That these representations are based on bottom-up (i.e., perceptually driven) processes rather than top-down (i.e., conceptually driven) ones is evidenced by the fact that the categories infants form are susceptible to subtle changes in the surface features of the stimuli (French, Mareschal, Mermillod, & Quinn, 2004).

Infants are also highly sensitive to the statistical regularities to which they are exposed across a range of perceptual inputs (e.g., Kirkham, Slemmer, & Johnson, 2002; Saffran, Aslin, & Newport, 1996). Consequently, it is thought that infants' initial categories are formed on the basis of correlations—or bundles—of static features. As evidence of this ability, Younger and colleagues (Younger, 1990; Younger & Cohen, 1986; Younger & Gotlieb, 1988) have shown that, across a variety of experimental paradigms, 10-month-old infants are sensitive to correlated features in a category context for artificial animal stimuli, as well as realistic color photographs of animals. Thus, the first representations for objects and entities primarily involve correlations among the surface, static features of objects; that is, they encapsulate how things look.

How Things Move: Dynamic Cues

There is considerably less agreement about when and how infants learn about the motion properties of things. Of issue is how infants incorporate information about dynamic cues into their already existing static feature-based representations and the mechanisms that underpin this learning. We use the terms *dynamic cues* and *dynamic features* here to refer to the movement or change in state of an object or entity or of any of its properties; those aspects of objects that cannot be extracted from a single frame. Dynamic stimuli could be visual (e.g., the path of an object as it moves from point A to point B) or auditory (e.g., the barking of a dog or the word "furniture"). To demarcate dynamic features further, we use *local dynamic cues* to refer to the movement of object features (e.g., a mouth, legs, wheels) and *global dynamic cues* to refer to the motion of an object across space or the role it may play in an event (e.g., linear movement from point A to point B or acting as an agent in a causal scene). Note that our claim is not that

3

static and dynamic features are represented differently; instead, we propose that all features are represented via the same learning mechanism and are represented in fundamentally similar ways.

Dynamic features—specifically those related to the motion properties of animates and inanimates—are difficult for infants to learn for a number of reasons. They are available only intermittently in the perceptual input, which means that infants will learn about them more slowly than about static ones. Dynamic cues can also be vague and sometimes even deceptive, such as when a ball moves nonlinearly or appears to act as a causal agent (Gelman et al., 1995). Finally, such cues are inherently more difficult to process than static ones precisely because their dynamic nature makes them more complex; for example, static features—such as the legs of a stationary dog—are more readily encoded than dynamic features (e.g., a dog and its legs as it walks) because the latter must be tracked as they change in state over time.

We are not suggesting, however, that motion per se makes perceptual information more difficult to encode; there are numerous examples in the literature that motion can convey structure, which in turn makes the representation load lighter rather than heavier (see e.g., Gibson, 1966). Instead, our claim is that greater information-processing abilities are required to encode the global and local dynamic cues of things than to encode their static cues. We also recognize that at a low-enough level, all information is dynamic, unfolding in time as patterns of neural activity. Information from static scenes is subject to eye, head, and body movements and to neural stochasticity and so is by no means literally static. Here, we define static parts of an object as those that do not move in a principled way—what one would call stationary in ordinary language (eye movements notwithstanding). Dynamic parts are those moving in a principled way—what one would refer to as a moving part or object.

How Infants Represent Dynamic Cues: Domain-Specific Solutions

According to some theoretical frameworks, the complex nature of the problem space implies that the associative processes that allow infants to represent static features are insufficient to account for how they acquire concepts that include motion characteristics. It has been argued, for example, that associated percepts that involve motion—as well as some other basic spatial information such as support and containment—cannot lead to concepts that are accessible and support inference, thought, or recall (Mandler, 2003). A more general criticism is that associative learning alone cannot act as the foundation for early representations because of an *insufficiency of constraints*. The crux of this argument of *Original Sim* (Keil, 1981) is that there are so many correlations to which one could attend that it is impossible to know which ones are important for category membership and which are not.

As a solution to these and other issues, a number of theoretical frameworks have proposed that representations that incorporate the motion properties of animates and inanimates are acquired via innate specialized processes, innate knowledge or constraints, or evolved modules. A corollary of this perspective is that infants are viewed as precocious concept-formers with information about motion properties represented within the first year of life (e.g., Leslie, 1995; Mandler, 1992; Gelman, 1990; Premack, 1990; Spelke, 1994). These formulations differ considerably in their relative stress on the role of learning versus innate knowledge; but they all contrast with the domain-general framework proposed in this monograph.

Core Knowledge Approaches

One such group of theorists, loosely grouped together under the *core knowledge* view, have proposed that infants' understanding of the motion of objects and entities in the world is built on certain principles that are present at birth (e.g., Baillargeon, 2001; Baillargeon, Kotovsky, & Needham, 1995; Spelke, 1994; Spelke, Breinlinger, Macomber, & Johnson, 1992). These theorists focus predominantly on the rules and constraints that govern the motion of inanimate objects, and some also suggest that a separate module exists for reasoning about constraints on human action (Kuhlmeier, Wynn, & Bloom, 2004; Spelke & Kinzler, 2007; Spelke, Phillips, & Woodward, 1995). The essence of these views is that initial knowledge concerning inanimate objects' motion is constrained by innate principles about the laws of physics and that this knowledge becomes enriched through experience although the core concepts remain fundamentally the same throughout childhood and beyond. We agree with the idea that knowledge becomes enriched through experience; however, we provide an alternative for the idea that innate knowledge, modules, or specialized mechanisms are necessary to account for early learning about how things in the world move.

A good example of this view is the theory of R. Gelman (1990; R. Gelman et al., 1995). She proposed that infants are born with innate *skeletal causal principles* that engender the ability to develop conceptual schemes for objects and entities by guiding attention to aspects of their motion and composition and in particular the energy sources and materials that relate to those characteristics. Gelman (1990; Gelman, Durgin, & Kaufman, 1995) stressed that these skeletal causal principles are not a fully fledged conceptual understanding of a domain but that they involve some initial knowledge that directs later learning. Similarly, Leslie (1994, 1995) theorized that infants possess three innately derived modules that, in combination, allow infants to rapidly develop an understanding of the physical (*theory of body*), psychological (*theory of mind*), and cognitive properties of

5

animates and inanimates. Leslie (1994) proposed that each module consists of a specialized learning mechanism, a means of organizing input, and a means of acquiring information. It is unclear, though, how the kinds of modules or mechanisms proposed by Leslie are "triggered" by certain kinds of input but not others, especially when events involve both physical and psychological causality.

One of the most influential core knowledge theories was developed by Spelke (1994, Spelke et al., 1992, 1995). According to Spelke and colleagues, key innate principles relating to object motion are *continuity, solidity,* and *contact,* with other physical concepts (e.g., gravity and inertia) developing through experience on the basis of these core concepts. Although Spelke does not apply this theory directly to infants' knowledge of animate motion, the core principle of *contact*—whereby a physical object moves only following contact from another object—could be applied to learning about, for example, self-propulsion; infants would determine which things in the world start to move when no causal contact is present. More recently this view has been expanded to include the possibility that infants possess core knowledge in the domain of animate objects. For example, based on studies that tested 7-month-olds' understanding of self-propulsion, Markson and Spelke (2006) concluded that core knowledge principles may enable infants to learn and reason about various motion properties of things that behave or look like animals. We will demonstrate in this monograph, however, that a domain-general learning mechanism is sufficient to learn about self-propulsion as well as other motion characteristics of animates and inanimates.

Baillargeon presented a similar core knowledge view to Spelke but proposed that infants possess innate primitive concepts that are enriched through experience. To our knowledge, Baillargeon has not specified the nature and content of these initial concepts, though she has proposed a specialized learning mechanism that enhances infants' physical knowledge based on experience (Baillargeon, 1995, 1998, 1999, 2001; Baillargeon et al., 1995). Baillargeon subsequently refined this theory to incorporate an "incremental knowledge" account of the acquisition of physical knowledge in infancy (Baillargeon, 2001, 2004; Luo & Baillargeon, 2005).

This more recent account, which overlaps somewhat with an information-processing perspective, was developed to explain how infants succeed in visual tasks involving certain motion events but fail in other, more complex events. Baillargeon suggested that categories for events have *vectors,* or elements, that must be predicted for an infant to understand the event appropriately. In an occlusion event, for example, infants must predict when an object will reappear from behind an occluder (Wang, Baillargeon, & Paterson, 2005). The products of vectors are ascertained through *variables,* which are a set of outcome-rules that allow infants to determine the vector information more accurately. For an occlusion event, variable information might include outcome-rules relating to the object's speed before it traveled behind the occluder as well as the width of the occluder. Initially, infants can represent only basic information about an event and not the variable information; for instance, they can represent the number of objects in the event, their geometry, and spatial arrangement. In this way, infants possess basic innate knowledge of constraints on the motions of objects and it becomes refined over developmental time. We view this part of Baillargeon's work as commensurate with aspects of the framework proposed here, though we shall show that the strength of connections in an associative network, and not outcome-rules, are sufficient for this kind of learning.

Baillargeon, like Spelke, has only recently begun to apply this view to how infants acquire concepts for the motions of animate objects. For example, based on findings that 5-month-old infants attribute goal-directed action to inanimate objects, she proposed that the ability to reason about goals is based on a specialized system that is "activated when infants attempt to predict and interpret the actions of entities they identify as agents" (Luo & Baillargeon, 2005, p. 607). Yet the existence of such a specialized system is inferential and other researchers have applied a more domain-general interpretation of infants' understanding of goal-directed action within the first year of life (Woodward, 1998, 1999; see also Baldwin, Baird, Saylor, & Clark, 2001).

Mandler's Theory: Perceptual Analysis

According to Mandler's (1992, 2000, 2003) prominent theory, infants possess an innate specialized process called *perceptual analysis* that recodes the perceptual display into an abstract and accessible construct. This process generates *image-schemas*, or *conceptual primitives*, that summarize crucial characteristics of objects' spatial structure and movement. Image schemas for animates, for example, include self-motion and the capacity to cause action at a distance, whereas image schemas for inanimates include caused-motion and motion caused through contact.

Mandler (1992) argued that although infants' first concepts are grounded in the surface appearance of things, which allow *perceptual categorization*, by around 12 months of age image schemas provide infants with an understanding of the *meaning* of things (what Mandler calls *conceptual categorization*). Thus, 3-month-olds may categorize different dogs as equivalent because of their surface features (Eimas & Quinn, 1994) but 12-month-olds will categorize the same dogs as equivalent because of an understanding that they are self-propelled entities that can act as agents. According to Mandler, perceptual and conceptual categorization involves two separate but connected processes; during perceptual categorization things are recognized by their surface appearance and during conceptual categorization they are classified because of their motion characteristics or category relatedness, or in other words, their *meaning*. Unfortunately, Mandler has never tested empirically whether the bases for induction and categorization are abstract concepts that encapsulate how things move. Indeed, a number of researchers have reported data that bring into question a rich interpretation of infants' behavior in experimental tasks (e.g., Behl-Chadha, 1996; Oakes & Cohen, 1990; Rakison, 2005b; Rakison & Butterworth, 1998; Younger & Johnson, 2004).

Critique of the Domain-Specificity Approach

Consistent with these core knowledge frameworks, we stress the acquisition of motion properties in the early development of concepts for objects and entities. However, there are a number of reasons—both theoretical and empirical—to question whether innate specialized modules, knowledge, or mechanisms are necessary to account for this learning. First, there is no direct empirical evidence that infants possess innate modules, innate core knowledge, or specialized mechanisms that allow them to encode distinct kinds of information (and in particular, motion characteristics). Indeed, the very notion of an innate specialized module or a core principal is difficult, if not impossible, to test empirically. Two lines of reasoning that are commonly adopted by core knowledge theorists are that if an ability or knowledge is present early in life it must be innate and that if infants find certain expectations—about, for example, continuity—difficult to learn then these expectations may be innate (see e.g., Baillargeon, 1999; c.f., Haith, 1998). Both of these assumptions logically are flawed: if infants display knowledge about an event at 3 months of age, they have had 3 months to learn about such events; if infants find it difficult to form an expectation for an event it does not necessarily mean that it is not learned. Second, the notion that infants possess two separate mechanisms for concept formation—one for perceptual information and one for conceptual information (Mandler, 1992)—has been labeled as unparsimonious because it creates a heavy biological burden (Madole & Oakes, 1999; Quinn & Eimas, 2000; Quinn, Johnson, Mareschal, Rakison, & Younger, 2000; Rakison & Hahn, 2004). Third, although we agree that motion cues can be misleading (Gelman et al. 1995), there may well be sufficient regularities in the world for an associative mechanism to account for learning in this domain (see later in this chapter for details). Fourth, in the absence of empirical evidence it remains unspecified how a specialized process—for example, perceptual analysis or that posited by Baillargeon—abstracts dynamic, motion-related information into a simpler, more available form or whether such a process is different from perceptual categorization of movement patterns (Quinn & Eimas, 2000; Rakison, 2003).

Finally, current accounts do not present a developmental perspective on early concept formation. This is not to say that domain-specific views overlook development entirely; but none of the described frameworks explain how or why infants' ability to form representations incorporating motion (and other properties) improves over time.

THEORETICAL FRAMEWORK

As an alternative to these previous views, we present here a theoretical framework that has at its core the idea that general rather than specific mechanisms are sufficient to account for how infants incorporate the motion properties of objects and entities into their developing concepts. In particular, we propose that infants develop representations for animates and inanimates that include both static and dynamic cues through a domain-general process called *constrained attentional associative learning* (Rakison, 2005a, 2006), abbreviated here as CAAL. The fundamental features of this framework are the following:

1. The primary mechanism that supports early concept formation is domain-general associative learning.

2. Conceptual development is best depicted as a continuous incremental augmentation of initial representations.

3. Infants possess a number of inherent perceptual biases that direct attention to specific aspects of the array.

4. There exist sufficient statistical regularities regarding static and dynamic cues within the category of animates and the category of inanimates.

5. The development of object concepts is explained by advances in information-processing abilities such as improving short- and long-term memory and increasing encoding speed, as well as neurological maturation.

6. Constraints on learning emerge as a product of prior experience with statistical regularities.

It is now well established that associative processes are an important part of infants' ability to represent the world around them (e.g., Fiser & Aslin, 2001, 2002; Gogate & Bahrick, 1998; Kirkham, Slemmer, & Johnson,

2002; Madole & Cohen, 1995; Rakison, 2004, 2005a, 2006; Slater, Mattock, Brown, Burnham, & Young, 1991; Younger & Cohen, 1986). We propose that such processes are primary to developing conceptual knowledge about the static and dynamic characteristics of things in the world. In particular, we argue that infants' first representations for the objects and entities they encounter involve encoding individual and correlated static features such as, in the case of dogs for example, eyes, legs, tails, and mouths. Later, as the representational system becomes capable of encoding more complex dynamic information—largely as a result developing more sophisticated information-processing abilities—concepts for objects and entities will begin to include intermittently available information such as those relating to motion (e.g., things with legs are self-propelled).

This association between an object part and an object motion allows infants to categorize and make inductive inferences on the basis of object properties not available in the perceptual input. For example, infants do not have to observe an animal with moving legs to treat it as a self-propelled entity; instead, the observation that an object possesses legs leads to the *expectation* that it will engage in specific kinds of motions. With the addition of other, perhaps less causally relevant features to this initial relation, and later with the emergence of labeling, the associative link expands to include a multitude of features as well as whole objects and categories of objects. At the same time, these learned associations act to constrain the other associations to which infants attend and encode.

In the sections that follow, we describe the theoretical and empirical support for the features of the theory. We then present a connectionist simulation that incorporates these features to model infant behavior in learning about objects' motion trajectory, their causal role, their onset of motion, and the initial mapping between a label and a dynamic object. We also present empirical data with infants that tested predictions generated by the model with regard to learning verbal labels.

The Primary Mechanism That Supports Early Concept Formation Is Domain-General Associative Learning

One of our primary claims is that the mechanisms that underlie early object concept formation are general rather than specialized. The term *domain-general* is used here to refer to learning processes that operate on a range of inputs—for example, auditory, visual, and tactile stimuli—and that are not context or information specific. These mechanisms include, but are not limited to, associative learning, classical and operant conditioning, habituation, and imitation. The framework presented here stresses associative learning; however, it should be noted that we acknowledge that these other general processes likely facilitate infants' representational development.

Associative learning is an outstanding candidate as the cornerstone mechanism for early representational development of the static and dynamic properties of things in the world because it has been shown to operate powerfully across a range of input domains and stimulus types. As described earlier, by 7–10 months of age infants are adept at extracting correlational information about the features of animals from a static input (e.g., Younger & Cohen, 1986). Perhaps highlighting the fundamental nature of associative learning, there is also evidence that the ability to encode correlations among features is present at birth. Slater et al. (1991), for example, found that newborns familiarized to stimulus compounds—such as a green vertical stripe and a red diagonal stripe—encoded the relation between the two features (color and slant) rather than each feature independently.

There is also evidence that associative learning allows infants to represent dynamic information involving not only objects' form but also their functional and linguistic features. Madole and colleagues (Madole, Oakes, & Cohen, 1993; Madole & Cohen, 1995), for example, used the "Switch" design to examine infants' ability to learn the relation between an object's form and its function. In the Switch design, attribute A^1 is paired with attribute B^1 in one habituation trial, and attribute A^2 is paired with attribute B^2 in another habituation trial. In Madole et al.'s (1993) studies, for instance, one attribute in each trial was an object feature (e.g., the color or appearance of the wheels) and the other was a function (e.g., whether or not the wheels could roll). In the test phase of the study, infants are shown one trial in which the attribute pairings presented during habituation are violated—attribute A^1 with attribute B^2, for example—and another in which the attribute pairings are identical to that presented earlier. In this design, recovery of visual attention to the switch test trial relative to the familiar test trial can only result from detection of a new attribute pairing rather than the introduction of a novel attribute. The results of the studies by Madole et al. (1993) showed that 18-month-olds, but not 14-month-olds, can learn the correlation between the form of an object and a particular dynamic function. A follow-up study by Madole and Cohen (1995) revealed that 14-month-olds will learn relations between form and function that do not make sense in the real-world (such as when the form of a part predicts the function of another part), whereas 18-month-olds will learn only those correlations that make sense in the real-world. This suggests that by 18 months infants bring to the laboratory knowledge about the relation between an object's part and its function. There is also evidence of a similar developmental trajectory when infants learn about the identity of objects that play different roles in causal events (Rakison, 2005a) and engage in self-propelled motion (Rakison, 2006).

11

Using similar designs, researchers have investigated infants' ability to attend to relations between auditory and visual information. Gogate and Bahrick (1998) showed that infants as young as 7 months are sensitive to arbitrary intermodal relations, such as the relationship between temporally synchronous vocalizations and moving objects, but only in the presence of a *facilitating cue* such as temporal synchrony, intensity shift, or common rhythm. By the second year of life, these cues are no longer necessary; however, Werker et al. (1998), for example, used the Switch design in a habituation procedure to show that in the absence of temporal synchrony 14-month-olds associate a label (e.g., "Neem") with an object (e.g., a dog) when the object in question moves.

These studies are generally consistent with the view that associative learning is a domain-general mechanism that has the potential to support infant concept development across a range of static and dynamic inputs. The literature suggests that infants are sensitive to correlations among static cues in the first year of life but that, in the absence of certain facilitating cues, they do not show sensitivity to relations among dynamic cues involved in object motion until approximately 14 months of age. It is in this age range, then, that the ability to associate specific motion properties with specific objects or entities should emerge. As a corollary, at some point after this age infants should demonstrate knowledge of the relation between the way an object moves and the features that it possesses.

Conceptual Development Is Best Depicted as a Continuous Incremental Augmentation of Initial Representations

Our general theoretical view of conceptual development is similar to a number of other proposals that have associative learning at their forefront (e.g., Colunga & Smith, 2005; Quinn & Eimas, 1997) in that we offer that concept acquisition in infancy and beyond is a process of continuous representational augmentation. By this we mean that infants' initial representations accrue in a gradual manner as ever more detailed and rich information about the world is encoded. This perspective differs from classic stage-based theories proposed by Piaget and Kohlberg, as well as more recent accounts such as those by Carey (1985) and Wellman (1990). However, the view is consistent with an increasingly large database of developmental data, as well as a recent theoretical shift that views development not as a set of discrete "jumps" from one state to another but rather as an increase and decrease in the frequency with which certain strategies, information, or processes are relied upon (Jones & Smith, 1993; Madole & Oakes, 1999; Quinn & Eimas, 1997; Siegler, 1996). According to our framework, during infancy and early childhood (at least) representations undergo quantitative rather than qualitative change, with abrupt, stage-like changes in behavior resulting from the continuing addition of information to already established representations. The connectionist model presented in the following chapters provides a demonstration of this kind of change (see also Schafer & Mareschal, 2001).

Although previous theoretical accounts for concept development have adopted a similar perspective, the specifics varied considerably, and none sufficiently accounted for how infants learn about the motion properties of things in the world. Table 1 presents a summary of these and other domain-specific theoretical views on early concept development, and it highlights whether these theories have empirically tested predictions relating to motion or developed a computational model of their account.

One of the most influential theories emphasizing continuity was developed by Linda Smith and colleagues (Jones & Smith, 1993; Smith, Jones, & Landau, 1996; Smith, Colunga, & Yoshida, 2003; Smith & Heise, 1992). Smith's framework focuses on early feature and word learning whereby infants' experience with word–object correlations in the world leads them to attend to the features that are a part of those correlations. According to this perspective, naming automatically directs attention to certain object properties (e.g., shape) because of the associations they have learned previously (Samuelson & Smith, 1999; Smith et al., 1996; Colunga & Smith, 2005); attention to shape over texture causes the representational space for shape to become closer while at the same time creating distance in the representational space for texture. This leads infants to rely on shape rather than texture as the basis for generalization in the course of labeling, for example. Smith and colleague have not, however, directly addressed how infants learn about the motion properties of objects.

Quinn and Eimas (Eimas, 1994; Quinn & Eimas, 1996, 1997, 2000) presented a related framework for category and concept development, but they focused on infants' initial representation of the static features of objects and entities. As we do, Quinn and Eimas proposed that concept development is a process of continuous representational enrichment grounded in a perceptual system that is sufficiently sensitive to allow infants to form categories that cohere because of perceptible similarity relations. In support of this view, Quinn, Eimas, and colleagues have generated a large database that attests to the fact that infants in the first 7 months of life categorize successfully objects and entities (presented as pictures) from a variety of basic- and superordinate-level contrasts on the basis of surface features.

Their findings (Quinn & Eimas, 1997, 2000) have documented that infants in the first year of life may include self-initiated biological motion in their concepts of humans and animals. Quinn and Eimas further proposed that the onset of language comprehension and production facilitates acquisition of knowledge about the less observable characteristics of objects (in particular, biological functions such as reproduction and other internal

TABLE 1

SUMMARY OF THE MAIN THEORETICAL VIEWS OF CONCEPT DEVELOPMENT IN INFANCY

	General framework for infants' learning about motion	Domain-general or domain-specific account?	Framework tested empirically with infants?	Implemented as a computational model?
Mandler (1992)	Specialized process called perceptual analysis recodes motion information into a conceptual format	Domain-specific	No experiments involving motion	No
Gelman (1990)	Skeletal causal principles contain initial knowledge that guides later learning of motion	Domain-specific	Experiments with preschoolers but not infants	No
Leslie (1995)	Three modules process the mechanical, goal-directed, and cognitive behavior of Agents	Domain-specific	Experiments with infants but no evidence to support modular view	No
Eimas & Quinn (1997)	Information involving motion is "abstracted" by general learning processes	Domain-general	Experiments with young infants but only with static images	Yes, but only for infants' learning of static features
Jones & Smith (1993)	Unspecified. However, learning feature correlations increases attention to those correlations	Domain-general	Experiments mostly involve word learning	Yes, but only for infants' word learning
Rakison & Lupyan	General learning mechanisms lead causal features of objects to be associated with specific motions	Domain-general	Experiments with infants directly testing hypotheses	Yes, includes static and dynamic features, and labels

properties) through formal and informal tuition. They argued, therefore, that language functions "as an input system that can serve as a rich source of information about objects that may not often, or even ever, be immediately apparent through looking, hearing, touching, and tasting" (Quinn & Eimas,

2000, p. 57). The combination of linguistic input, along with the continuous enrichment of perceptually based representations, leads infants to form representations for animals that include shape, texture, facial features, and motion properties as well as less directly perceptible properties. The details of how this process might operate with respect to motion, however, have not been specified. Eimas (1994; see also Quinn & Eimas, 1997), for instance, stated that, "The common aspects of the features for animate things, for example, biological motion ... are presumed to be recognized and abstracted" (p. 87).

We concur that the same basic processes are involved in representing object features and object motion. However, it is ambiguous how this process of "abstraction" might operate, or even what exactly is meant by the term "abstraction" in this context. Mandler (1992) suggested that the process of perceptual analysis recodes the perceptual display into an abstract and more accessible form, but perceptual analysis was hypothesized as a specialized process that evolved precisely to perform this task. Quinn and Eimas (1997), in contrast, did not specify how abstraction of motion properties, in particular, occurs within an associative learning framework. We propose that motion cues are not "abstracted" in the way described by Quinn and Eimas (1997; Eimas, 1994), but instead infants initially associate specific motion properties with specific object features (e.g., legs and self-propulsion) and later generalize this association to other object features not causally related to the motion (e.g., eyes). We also differ from Quinn and Eimas (1997) in our view of how the introduction of labels changes infants' representations.

Infants Possess a Number of Inherent Perceptual Biases That Direct Attention to Specific Aspects of the Array

One issue that is not addressed in previous associative learning formulations is why infants initially attend to some correlations in the world and ignore others. Any theory of object concept development must account for how infants attend to motion cues, which ones they may find especially salient, and why might they associate some object features with specific motion characteristics (for in depth discussions of these issues see Granrud, 1993). Quinn and Eimas (1997) point out that some static features may be more salient than others and therefore may be at the core of early representations; however, to our knowledge they have presented no formalized framework that explains the relative salience of different static cues and provide no discussion of the salience of dynamic, motion-related cues.

In our view infants possess a number of attention biases that early in life (and beyond in some cases) elevate the salience of particular aspects of the array (Rakison, 2003, 2004; Rakison & Hahn, 2004). We use the term

15

inherent here to highlight the fact that these biases are present at birth or shortly thereafter and that although they require input to be activated they are not an emergent property of learning. We regard these simple biases as evolved adaptations that are part of the human visual system and are shared with other animals. There is evidence, for example, that infants and newly hatched chicks show a spontaneous preference for motion (e.g., Slater, 1989; Vallortigara, Regolin, & Marconato, 2005). The presence of such biases in human infants increases the likelihood that certain aspects of the environment will be encoded. Based on the available empirical evidence, much of it involving newborns, we suggest that attention biases direct infants to attend to relatively large stimuli over relatively small ones (Slater, Mattock, & Brown, 1990), relatively complex over relatively simple stimuli (Kaplan & Werner, 1986), individual object features (Younger & Cohen, 1986), as well as simple face-like stimuli (Johnson & Morton, 1991) and that these biases facilitate the development of object concepts.

As described above, an additional bias that is primary for our account is that infants are more likely to attend to dynamic cues than static cues (Slater, 1989). A large literature attests that very young infants are drawn to moving stimuli and that, in some cases, their learning is facilitated in the presence of dynamic rather than static cues. For example, young infants learn relations among dynamic cues in studies that involve conditioning (e.g., 3-month-olds learn to kick their legs to make a mobile move, Hayne, 1996) as well as in the presence of a *facilitating cue* such as, in the case of sound and object relations, temporal synchrony, intensity shift, or common rhythm (Gogate & Bahrick, 1998). Infants in the first year of life are also sensitive to point-light displays for animals and vehicles (Arterberry & Bornstein, 2002), though it is possible that responses to such stimuli were based on perceptual categorization of circular versus pendulum motion rather than the ability to encode correlations among dynamic cues.

By our account, however, it is not until the second year of life that infants start to learn about the dynamic properties—and in particular those involving global motion—of animals, vehicles, people, and other animates and inanimates. The rationale for this view is that although dynamic information is highly salient, it requires considerable information-processing abilities to track and encode an object's static and dynamic features as they move. In support of this view, it has been found that it is not until approximately 10 months of age that infants are able to integrate relatively complex information over space and time (Arterberry, 1993; Rose, Gottfried, Melloy-Carminar, & Bridger, 1982). Moreover, recent research on object motion (e.g., causality, self-propulsion) that examined the ability to encode features as they change across space and time have consistently shown that it is not until the end of the first year, or thereafter, that infants are capable of learning under such conditions (Rakison, 2004, 2005a, 2006).

16

To be clear, our claim is not that infants in the first year of life are insensitive to dynamic cues—indeed there is substantial evidence to show that this is not the case and that motion can attract infants' attention which means they are more likely to encode this information (for a discussion, see Nelson, 1973). For example, Robinson and Sloutsky (2004) found that infants as young as 8 months of age selectively attend to and remember dynamic auditory cues rather than static visual cues, and Horst, Oakes, and Madole (2005; see also Perone & Oakes, 2006) found that 10-month-olds learn the function of objects (e.g., a hand shaking an object that rattles) as well as their surface, static appearance. More impressive, perhaps, infants are able to learn an important aspect of animacy—namely, that hands are goal-directed—as early as 5 months of age (Woodward, 1998; see also Baldwin et al., 2001). However, in all of these experiments the dynamic features involved were intermittently available in the input (i.e., a sound or a function) and encoding them did not require the infant to attend to and encode an object across time and space. For instance, in the work by Woodward (1998), in which a hand was seen to reach toward one of two objects, 5-month-old infants needed only to attend to the final resting place of the hand and not to its motion trajectory.

It may well be that which features infants learn first depends on a complex interaction of competition between different features or stimuli, the information processing demands of learning each kind of set of features, and the salience of different features. It is difficult, however, to make static and dynamic features psychophysically equivalent—both in terms of their ability to capture attention, and in terms of the differences between stimuli that are being tested (though see Kaldy, Blaser, & Leslie (2006) for an ingenious method of calibrating equivalence for color and luminescence). It may well be that dynamic features are more salient than static features, but the discrimination between different dynamic feature values may be more difficult than the discrimination between different static feature values. It might be predicted, for instance, that infants would be able to learn highly discriminable dynamic aspects of motion (e.g., horizontal vs. vertical movement) within the first year of life (e.g., Wattam-Bell, 1996). Thus, we acknowledge that infants are capable of processing various dynamic cues toward the end of the first year of life, and that the story is more complex than a static-to-dynamic learning pattern. At the same time, however, we suggest that it is not until approximately 10–12 months of age that they are able to encode relations among dynamic cues that involve relatively complex information related to motion characteristics of object and entities (e.g., agency, self-propulsion).

We posit that the biases outlined above help to direct infants' attention to information that differentiates animates from inanimates. Specific surface features of people, animals, and certain vehicles (e.g., hand, legs, arms, wings, wheels) tend to move concurrently as they exhibit specific motions; thus, if the attentional system is directed toward objects and object features as, and because, they move, infants will associate the movement of the feature with the specific motion characteristic displayed (see also Rogers & McClelland, 2004). To give a more concrete example: When a dog starts to move without external force—that is, when it engages in self-propulsion—its legs also start to move. If an infant's attention is directed to these dynamic features, an associative learning mechanism could encode the relation between the global (self-propulsion) and the local (legs) movement in the perceptual array. Direct support for this view was found in the studies by Rakison and colleagues (Rakison, 2004, 2005a, 2006; Rakison & Poulin-Dubois, 2002) in which infants encoded relations between dynamic cues (i.e., a moving part and an object's motion trajectory) and ignored other relations involving static cues (i.e., those involving the body of the object) or failed to encode correlations among parts and a dynamic trajectory when the parts did not move. Inanimate objects, in contrast to animate entities, tend not to show evidence of such relations between dynamic cues even when they possess dynamic features (e.g., a clock's hands); when a mug is caused to move by a person, there is no change in state of the features of the mug. This means that infants may well learn that there exists a relation between animate-like object parts (e.g., legs, wings) and specific animate motions but that this relation does not exist for inanimates.

There Exist Sufficient Statistical Regularities Regarding Static and Dynamic Cues Within the Category of Animates and the Category of Inanimates

Naturally, an associative learning mechanism cannot underpin concept development for the static and dynamic aspects of animates and inanimates unless the input is sufficiently structured within each category. That is, there must be adequate statistical regularities in the world for an associative learning mechanism to make representational sense of it by extracting those regularities. Associative learning alone could not account for how infants learn about the motion properties of things if, for example, there is no relation between the features of animate entities and their global motions.

An informal consideration of the properties of animates and inanimates suggests that the input is indeed sufficiently structured in this way. As a starting point, it is worth considering the different ways in which animates and inanimates move. Based on earlier theoretical contributions by Gelman and Spelke (1981), Premack (1990), Mandler (1992), and Rakison and Poulin-Dubois (2001) proposed that seven motion characteristics help to delineate animates, on the one hand, and inanimates, on the other. These characteristics are presented in Table 2. Of issue is the extent to which these characteristics overlap across the categories of animates and inanimates.

TABLE 2

CHARACTERISTIC MOTIONS OF ANIMATES AND INANIMATES

Motion characteristic	Category	Typical motion	Crossover	Example
Onset of motion	Animate	Self-propelled	No	N/A
	Inanimate	Caused motion	Yes	A person pushes another
Line of trajectory	Animate	Irregular	Yes	A ball bounces
	Inanimate	Smooth	Yes	A person walks directly from point A to point B
Form of causal action	Animate	Action at a distance	No	N/A
	Inanimate	Action from contact	Yes	A person picks up a cat
Pattern of interaction	Animate	Noncontingent	No	N/A
	Inanimate	Contingent	Yes	A person imitates another
Type of causal role	Animate	Agent	No	N/A
	Inanimate	Recipient	Yes	A person hits another
Purpose of action	Animate	Goal-directed	No	N/A
	Inanimate	Aimless	Yes	A person walks through a park
Influence of mental states	Animate	Intentional	No	N/A
	Inanimate	Accidental	Yes	A person inadvertently drops an object

As can be seen, animates can engage in all seven of the motion characteristics listed as typical of inanimates. For example, people and animals can be self-propelled or move because of an external physical cause, and they can be the agent or recipient of a causal event.[1] Table 2 also shows that inanimates rarely perform animate-like motions, the exception being that some inanimates (e.g., balls, vehicles, leaves) can move nonlinearly as well as linearly.

The implication of this analysis is that infants will observe only animates engaging in animate-typical motion, whereas they may observe both animates and inanimates engaging in inanimate-typical motion. This suggests that there are structural regularities regarding the way different object kinds move in the world that could be used conceptually to demarcate animates from inanimates. In particular, the analysis suggests that motion properties may be more central, or defining, to the representation of animates than inanimates.

One way to test this prediction is by examining the semantic feature production norms generated by McRae, Cree, Seidenberg, and McNorgan (2005) for 541 animates and inanimates. The norms were created by asking approximately 725 adult participants to list features for living and non-living things (presented as words). For each object, the participants were encouraged to list different types of features including physical properties,

19

functional properties, to which category it belongs, and any other encyclopedic facts. Moreover, for every concept, the features listed by participants were recorded along with their production frequency, which was defined as the number of participants who noted that feature for that concept (ranging between 1 and 30). The concepts in the corpus had been previously used in various experiments on semantic memory—including classic work by Rosch and Mervis (1975)—with both normal adults and psychological patients. The aim was to include concepts that cover a broad range of living and nonliving things that varied in familiarity to the participants.

The full set of norms may be downloaded from www.psychonomic.org/archive/. Because of the extensive depth provided by the norms, they can be used to calculate a range of measures and distributional statistics including estimates of feature saliency (production frequency, cue validity) as well as measures of how various features are distributed across concepts. Because these norms were generated by adults, they reflect an adult-level understanding of the world, yet many of the features that were generated such as "has teeth" or "can swim" are easily available from the perceptual input. Clearly, however, caution must be adopted before making strong claims from these norms about the nature and content of infants' concepts.

For the purposes of this monograph, we focused predominantly on three aspects of the norms for animates versus inanimates. We examined the number of visual-motor features for each concept, the number of visual form and surface features for each concept, and the number of functional features for each concept. The concept "alligator," for example, lists two visual-motor features (swims and eats people), six visual form and surface features (e.g., has teeth, has a tail), and no functional features. We first tested the prediction that motion properties are more central to the concepts for animates than inanimates by examining whether adults would more often list visual form and surface features related to motion for animates than for inanimates. To address this issue, we compared the number of visual-motor features listed for the 135 animates and for the 404 inanimates (two concepts, "bedroom" and "apartment" were deleted from the list because they were not objects in the same sense as the other concepts). As predicted, adult participants listed significantly more visual-motor features related to motion for animates ($M = 2.06$) than for inanimates ($M = 0.15$), $t(537) = 25.38$, $p < .0001$.

A corollary of our prediction is that adults should list more motion-related surface features for animates than inanimates. To test this, we compared the number of visual form and surface features listed in the norms that were specifically related to motion (e.g., has wings or has wheels but not has scales or has a siren). The analysis revealed that, as predicted, adults listed more motion-related surface features for animates ($M = 0.90$) than for inanimates ($M = 0.05$), $t(537) = 14.26$, $p < .0001$. As a follow-up analysis,

20

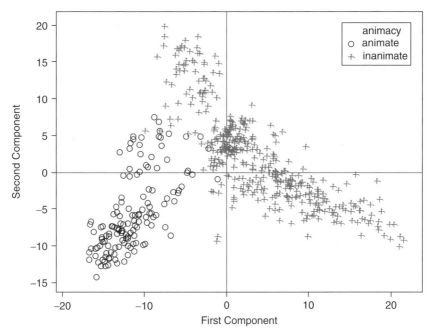

FIGURE 1.—Principal-component analysis on the between-concept cosine matrix for 539 concepts in the McRae et al. (2005) corpus.

we determined that the mean number of visual form and surface features for animates ($M = 4.41$) and inanimates ($M = 4.25$) did not differ significantly, $t(537) = 0.78$, $p > .4$. Thus, the difference between animates and inanimates in the number of surface features related to motion could not be attributed to the fact that more surface features were listed overall for animates than for inanimates.

As a next step we determined whether animacy is indeed a salient feature in concept representations. To address this question, we coded the animacy status of the 539 objects in the McRae et al. corpus (2005) and then performed a principal-component analysis on the between-concept cosine matrix for all the concepts. For instance, the entry for "alligator" had a value of 0 for "airplane" (i.e., alligators and airplanes shared no features produced by the raters), 0.13 for apple, 0.02 for axe, and so on. As Figure 1 shows, plotting the first two principal components reveals a clustering of animate and inanimate concepts. To quantify the degree to which the animacy distinction is represented in the correlation matrix, we then performed a K-means cluster analysis on the first 50 principal components of the matrix.[2] Of the 138 animate concepts, 134 (97%) were correctly classified. Of the 401 inanimate concepts, 398 (99%) were correctly classified, $\chi^2 = 502.80$, $p < .0005$. The animate concepts that were incorrectly classified by the algorithm were python, snail, worm, caterpillar, and clam, and the two misclassified inanimates were airplane and jet. Note that all the incorrectly classified animates lack legs and the incorrectly classified inanimates have movement as a prominent property—evidence that motion properties are critical to animacy. Additionally, we found that animates were more tightly grouped, having on average significantly smaller distances from the cluster centroid than inanimates: two-sample t-test not assuming equal variance, $t(352) = 14.11$, $p < .0005$.

To provide an additional confirmation of the idea that animacy is a salient factor in item concepts, we applied the same clustering procedure to representations of the same concepts derived from a completely different semantic corpus—the correlated occurrence analogs to lexical semantics (COALS: Rohde, Gonnerman, & Plaut, 2007; http://dlt4.mit.edu/ ~ dr/ COALS/). Rather than being based on features provided by human raters, the semantic representations in this corpus are generated automatically as the algorithm is trained on large amounts of text (the method is similar to HAL, developed by Lund and Burgess, 1996). The algorithm produces vectors with similarity relations based on the similarity of the contexts in which the words are used. Relationships between semantic vectors generated by the COALS method have been shown to correlate well with similarity ratings provided by human raters. Because corpus-based semantic representations cannot differentiate between homonyms, we removed words with obvious dual meanings (e.g., "bat"), and were left with 513 concepts. Applying K-means cluster analysis to the first 50 binary dimensions of the representations revealed that animacy was saliently represented. Of the 379 inanimate concepts, 316 (83%) were correctly classified. Of the 134 animate concepts, 119 (89%) were correctly classified, $\chi^2 = 225.3$, $p < .0005$. The animates were again found to be more tightly clustered than the inanimates, $t(176) = 6.71$, $p < .0005$. This lower, but still impressively high clustering performance results from analyzing 50 dimensional binary vectors (the full corpus contains 1,500 dimensions for each concept), and without relying on any explicitly generated features.

These analyses imply considerable statistical regularities between static and dynamic cues within the category of animates and the category of inanimates, and that adults' representation reflect these structural regularities. First, the data support the notion that motion properties are more central to the representations of animates than of inanimates. We argue, based on the analysis of Rakison and Poulin-Dubois's (2001) seven motion characteristics, that this pattern was found because motion properties are highly predictive that something is animate and considerably less so that something is inanimate. Second, the analyses reveal that representations for animates tend to stress features involved in motions (e.g., has legs, has wings) more so than for inanimates (for a similar view, see Smith et al.,

2003). Third, we showed that animacy is a salient feature in concept representations; that is, the distinction between animates and inanimates is a psychologically real one.

Development Is Explained by Advances in Information-Processing Abilities Such as Improving Short- and Long-Term Memory and Increasing Encoding Speed, as Well as Neurological Maturation

Thus far we have outlined a theory of concept development without a detailed discussion of how development itself occurs. The idea that concept formation is underpinned by associative processes coupled with inherent attention biases cannot, on its own, explain how infants represent distinct properties for objects and entities at different points in the first years of life. That is, it does not describe or explain how infants become able to encode ever more complex information over developmental time. Development, according to a number of theories, involves the "triggering" of modules or domain-specific processes by the appropriate input (e.g., Leslie, 1995; Mandler, 1992). Yet it remains to be seen how specific inputs trigger the appropriate module. In contrast to these perspectives, we propose that the basic mechanisms involved in concept development—including associative learning—do not change over time. Instead, our view is that infants are able to encode ever more complex information over time as a result of, initially, advances in information-processing abilities and an increasingly sensitive perceptual system and then, later, the emergence of linguistic skills. Naturally, other aspects of development also play a role in these cognitive advances; for example, infants' ability to use the social and emotional cues of others to direct attention increases significantly in the first two years, as do their motor abilities. For the sake of our model, however, we focus specifically on perceptual and cognitive advances that engender changes in infants' representational abilities.

This perspective is aligned with one of the "principles" of category and concept development outlined by Oakes and Madole (2003). They argued, as do we, that advances in motor, cognitive, and linguistic abilities lead to a broadening of the pool of features that infant can use in categorization. Regarding developmental changes in information-processing abilities more explicitly, they suggested that improvements in memory "should lead to changes in infants' ability to use features that require integrating information over space or time" (Oakes & Madole, 2003, p. 138). Although we concur with this general position, in our view it is important to specify in greater detail the developmental changes in perceptual and information-processing abilities that may influence early category and concept formation. Particularly important information-processing abilities for concept formation are short- and long-term memory and encoding, and advances

23

in these abilities would be expected to occur in parallel with changes in infants' ability to learn more complex information about objects and entities in the world.

There are several key transition points in this regard (for an excellent discussion, see Ruff & Rothbart, 1996). First, it is not until approximately 2–3 months of age that infants possess the requisite perceptual skills to learn about the features and properties of real-world objects. Thus, it is around this age that they begin visually to track moving objects more readily (Ruff, Saltarelli, Capozzoli, & Dubiner, 1992), and scan internal as well as external contours of objects (Salapatek, 1975). These changes are thought to result from a maturation of the visual system (including the retina), as well as a shift from subcortical to cortical control of attention (Johnson, 1990; Lewis, Maurer, & Brent, 1989).

A second key transition point in information-processing occurs around 8–12 months of age. Until this point, infants show a linear decrease with age in the amount of time that is required to familiarize or habituate to stimuli, a trend that is thought to result from increasing encoding speed and improved short-term memory (Colombo, 1993, 1995; Kagan, McCall, Reppucci, Jordan, Levine, & Minton, 1971; Ross-Sheehy, Oakes, & Luck, 2003). However, when infants are approximately 8–12 months of age they begin to look longer rather than shorter times at visual displays or at two real objects presented simultaneously (Bakeman & Adamson, 1984; Ruff & Saltarelli, 1993). Moreover, 8–12-month-olds can bind features for both simple dynamic stimuli as well as more complex static stimuli (e.g., Gogate & Bahrick, 1998; Oakes, Ross-Sheehy, & Luck, 2006; Younger & Cohen, 1986). According to Kagan and colleagues, this transition is due to increases in memory capacity, and in particular to improvements in retrieval such that infants start to use representations of past experiences to compare with their current experience (though see Rochat [2001] for an alternative explanation that the onset of crawling means it is less likely that infants will sit still during habituation and other experimental procedures).

There are a number of plausible neurological influences on this transition. First, it has been suggested that the ability to bind object features, and in particular those relating to identity and location, requires the integration of, and communication between, distinct neural pathways known as the dorsal and ventral streams. The ventral visual pathway—referred to as the "what" pathway—is thought to process information about the color, shape, and parts of objects, whereas the dorsal visual pathway—referred to as the "where" pathway—is thought to process information location and action (Milner & Goodale, 1995; Ungerleider & Mishkin, 1982). Milner and Goodale (1995) proposed that both streams process information about object features and spatial location but that the information is used differently by each stream. It has been suggested that 8–12-month-old infants' emerging ability to bind feature and location information in visual short-term memory as well as long-term memory results from the maturation of the neural mechanism connecting these two streams, perhaps involving the posterior parietal lobe (Chao & Martin, 2000; Oakes et al., 2006; Todd & Sirois, 2004; for a review see Kaldy & Sigala, 2004).

A second viable neural influence on this transition is the maturation of the hippocampus, which helps to bind inputs from multiple brain regions together into a durable memory trace (e.g., Squire, Knowlton, & Musen, 1993). Although much of the hippocampus matures early in the first year, a crucial connection between the parahippocampus and the hippocampus—the dentate gyrus—as well as the prefrontal cortex goes through significant maturation toward the end of the first year and most of the second year of life (Serres, 2001). Indeed, the numbers of synapses in these structures do not peak until 20–24 months of age, at which point they are functionally mature, though this is followed by considerable synaptic pruning (Goldman-Rakic, 1987; Huttenlocher & Dabholkar, 1997). Although electrophysiological evidence from infants on the maturation of the dentate gyrus is scarce, it has been strongly implicated in the development of encoding, storage, and retrieval of memory during this period (see Bauer, 2006, for review). In sum, although admittedly speculative, we suggest that strong influences on information-processing abilities during this phase may be the maturation of communication between "what" and "where" neural mechanisms as well as the prefrontal cortex and dentate gyrus.

A final information-processing transition in infancy, which is marked by significant behavioral changes, occurs at around 18 months of age. It is at this age that infants begin to show evidence of symbolic activity (underscored by pretend play) and increasing expectations about potential outcomes or "what 'might be'" and "what 'must have been'" (Meltzoff, 1990, p. 2). More importantly, perhaps, it is around 18 month of age that infants begin to learn and produce words at a more rapid rate, an increase known as the *naming spurt*. According to Ruff and Rothbart (1996), this transition phase results from the emergence of basic behavioral and neurological executive functions, which is supported by development of the lateral prefrontal cortex as well as the frontal cortex (Diamond, 1991). This higher level of control allows infants to use represented, rather than current, information to make decisions and to act. It may also allow infants to incorporate more readily new information about objects—and in particular, labels—into their already existing representation.

We suggest that these transition points—which are underpinned by improvements in encoding speed, memory retrieval, and executive functioning—parallel changes in infants' ability to encode various properties of things in the world. The maturation of the perceptual system corresponds with the age at which infants start to form categorical representations for complex static images such as cats and dogs (Quinn & Eimas, 1996; Quinn, Eimas, & Rosenkrantz, 1993). The period between 3 and 10 months of age, during which encoding speed and short-term memory are thought to develop significantly, presumably through experience and maturation, is marked by an ever improving ability to represent static features of objects and correlations among those features (e.g., Younger & Cohen, 1986) as well as correlations among often presented dynamic features in the context of a facilitating cue (e.g., Gogate & Bahrick, 1998).

The most crucial developmental period for our purpose is between 12 and 22 months of age, when infants' encoding speed continues to increase and their ability to retrieve information from long-term memory improves considerably. During this time infants are able to learn about the dynamic relations between distinct object parts, functions, and global motion characteristics, and they begin to use previously acquired knowledge of these relations to guide their expectations about future events (Madole & Cohen, 1995; Madole et al., 1993; Rakison, 2004, 2005a, 2006). Finally, the period after 18 months or so, in which infants acquire labels more rapidly, is reflected by infants' ability to encode dynamic cues and static cues in complex contexts for a wide range of motion properties and to recall motion properties for specific objects and object categories (Rakison, 2004, 2005a, 2005b). In our view, it is not happenstance that infants' emerging ability to encode dynamic visual cues coincides with the rapid improvement in label acquisition and production.

Not surprisingly, there is a dearth of empirical evidence that these changes in information-processing abilities and the maturation of specific neurological regions are causally related to developmental changes in infants' ability to learn about animates and inanimates. That these changes co-occur in developmental time suggests only that they may be related. It also remains to be seen to what extent experience and maturation play a role in these developments. Our view, however, is that advances in short-term memory, long-term memory, encoding speed, and neurological development are strong candidates as the underlying basis of the observed transition points in infants' ability to encode different kinds of properties (e.g., static cues and then later dynamic cues).

Constraints on Learning Emerge as a Product of Prior Experience With Statistical Regularities

A final tenet of our theoretical perspective concerns the way that learning itself guides future learning, or, to put it another way, that specific learning constraints in infancy emerge from previous experience. The crux of this idea is that once infants form associations between specific static and dynamic cues, these association act to constrain the aspects of the array to which infants attend in the future by automatically guiding attention to similar relations to the exclusion of others. Initially these strong representational links and the attentional constraints that they generate cannot be inhibited; yet later in developmental time the mechanism may become less automatic as young children develop more executive control over the aspects of the array to which they attend.

This view has much in common with that of Smith, Jones, and Landau (1996; Landau, Smith, & Jones, 1988) who suggested that word learning provides "on-the-job training" for attention. They argued that naming automatically directs, or fine tunes, children's attention to certain object properties (e.g., shape) because of the associations they have learned. In support of this claim, Smith, Jones, Landau, Gershkoff-Stowe, and Samuelson (2002) found that 17-month-olds who were taught the shape-label relation for novel objects in the laboratory showed the generalization that objects with the same name have the same shape. A similar and broader perspective was presented Rogers and McClelland (2004) who suggested that concepts are constrained by the *coherent covariation* of properties, with properties and items that are closely clustered influencing each other's representations and determining the basis for generalization.

One clear prediction of this general view is that infants should be initially unconstrained in the relations they will learn but then, following exposure to a structured input, should start to learn only those relations that are consistent with their previous experience. Evidence to support this view has emerged recently in a number of paradigms and across a range of modalities. Namy, Campbell, and Tomasello (2004), for example, showed that 18-month-old infants will learn both arbitrary and iconic gestures, whereas 24-month-old infants will learn only iconic ones. Likewise, Stager and Werker (1997) revealed that 8-month-olds can perform finer-grained phonemic discrimination than 14-month-olds, in all likelihood because 8-month-olds have less experience with the phonemes of their native lexicon than 14-month-olds. Finally, Rakison (2005a, 2006; see also Madole & Cohen, 1995) found the same developmental trend in a separate series of studies that examined when and how infants learn about the relation between a static or dynamic part and agency and self-propulsion. The consistency among the developmental trajectories found in these diverse domains, which is depicted in Figure 2 for learning about self-propulsion and agency, suggests they may all be grounded in the same general mechanism; namely, associative learning (Rakison, 2005a, 2006; see also Rogers, Rakison, & McClelland, 2004).

The idea that learning constraints for specific domains emerge through the process of learning conflicts considerably with the notion that constraints for those domains are built in at birth. Although the latter view is

27

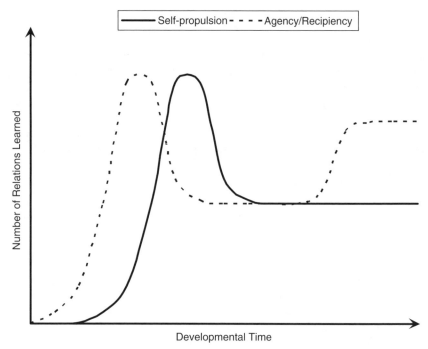

FIGURE 2.—Number of Relations Learned. Developmental trajectory for early learning about self-propulsion (based on the current experiments) and agency and recipiency (based on Rakison, 2005a). The figure demonstrates that infants are unable initially to encode certain relations, after which they are unconstrained in the relations to which they will attend. Prior experience then limits or guides attention to some relations and not others. Finally, for agency and recipiency these constraints must be relaxed to incorporate more accurately the state of relations in the world.

Note.—From Rakison (2006). Copyright © 2006 by the American Psychological Association. Reproduced with permission. The official citation that should be used in referencing this material is Rakison (2006). Make the first move: How infants learn about self-propelled objects, *Developmental Psychology, 42*, 900–912. The use of APA information does not imply endorsement by APA.

more often connected to the literature on language learning (for a review, see Markman, 1989), it is inherent in a number of theories relating to the development of concepts for animates and inanimates (e.g., Mandler, 1992; Spelke, 1994; Baillargeon, 2004). Frameworks that postulate innate modules, for example, imply that infants are automatically drawn to attend to, and to interpret, specific events in specific ways (e.g., Leslie, 1995; Premack, 1990). Models that involve innate specialized processes such as perceptual analysis imply that the process itself directs infants' attention to particular aspects of the array (e.g., motion). Crucially, however, these theories do not imply that infants' initially will be unconstrained in the relations they will learn, but later will be more limited in the information that they will encode. On the contrary, these frameworks suggest that by the end of the first year of life infants' representational system is fully functional and should constrain infant learning. As our brief review of the literature shows, however, this is not the case across a range of domains.

Summary of the Theoretical Framework

We have presented a framework, and supporting empirical evidence from the literature, for how infants develop representations for the perceptual, surface features and dynamic features of animates and inanimates. The key aspects of this framework, which we call *constrained attentional associative learning* (CAAL) (Rakison, 2005a, 2006), are the following: (1) domain-general associative processes are the fundamental mechanism for learning, (2) representations are continuously augmented over developmental time with more complex information, and (3) infants possess a number of inherent attention biases that early in life highlight specific aspects of the array. We also suggest that the categories of animates and inanimates are sufficiently rich in structure that associative mechanisms can extract the regularities that exist within them, that the driving force for development are advances in information-processing abilities such as long- and short-term memory and encoding speed, and that constraints on learning emerge from the process of learning itself.

NOTES

1. Note, however, that animates in all likelihood engage in animate-typical motion far more often than in inanimate-typical motion; people, for example, more often move without than because of an external physical cause. In addition, we are not claiming that inanimate objects never appear to engage in animate-like motion—a car may be self-propelled from an infant's perspective—but rather that there is a probabilistic relation between animates and a set of motion characteristics and inanimates and a different set of motion characteristics.

2. A *K*-means cluster analysis can be thought of as analysis of variance (ANOVA) in reverse. The clustering algorithm starts out with *k* random clusters (in the current case, animates and inanimates), and then attempts to minimize variability within each cluster while maximizing variability between clusters by moving items between the clusters. The analysis for which we report results involved seeding the clusters with a small number of known animate and inanimate items, and testing classification performance for the remainder of the items (see also Lupyan & Rakison, 2006).

II. A CONNECTIONIST MODEL FOR EARLY LEARNING ABOUT ANIMATES AND INANIMATES

In the simulations and experiments that follow, we implement the constrained attentional associative learning (CAAL) model according to the theoretical principles outlined above. Some of these features, such as inherent perceptual learning biases, are explicitly represented in the model, while others, such as domain-general associative learning, is a general feature of the connectionist architecture we employ. After implementing the model, we test its ability to account for infant learning about the static and dynamic properties of animate entities and inanimate objects.

The major reason for creating a computational account of a theory is that such implementations force the researcher to make explicit the assumptions embedded in the theoretical account (Hintzman, 1991). An assumption such as a "bias to attend to moving stimuli" can be made concrete by instantiating it in a computational model. A computational model offers three particular advantages over a verbal theory of the type presented in Chapter I. First, intuitions used to develop cognitive theories are often wrong, and even if correct can result in unexpected behavior (Hintzman, 1991). Second, implementing a theory in a computational model allows for a test of such intuitions in a formal context where the assumptions go beyond verbal labels. Third, a computational model can make concrete predictions that can be empirically tested. In the event the predictions are wrong, one can go back to the model and understand why it made the prediction and the assumptions that led to the incorrect prediction can be re-examined. Conversely, if the predictions of a model are correct one can examine what assumptions are central to the correct prediction. This mutual interaction between modeling and empirical data can reveal alternative explanations for experimental findings and unify disparate findings under a common framework (for a discussion, see McClelland, 1988).

IMPLEMENTING CAAL

The model of CAAL was implemented as a neural network, the task of which was to learn to represent items through a variant of auto-association. Auto-association is an error-driven learning process in which a network forms representations by learning to map input patterns onto themselves (Rumelhart, Hinton, & Williams, 1986). The error comes from the input pattern itself—in minimizing the error the network forms a representation across a hidden layer, the function of which is to recreate the original input. Because the error is derived from the input patterns themselves, the network is said to be self-supervised. With enough training and sufficient computational resources, such a network can learn a representation that can perfectly recreate the input patterns. Typically, however, both resources and training time are limited; thus, a network learns preferentially the features most important for representing the input space insofar as it can with the computational resources at its disposal.[3]

We chose to implement the CAAL framework using a connectionist architecture because we believe such an architecture is most closely aligned with the first feature of the theory: domain-general associative learning. An additional reason is that connectionist networks have been used to model a wide range of cognitive phenomena and they are familiar to many researchers (see Schlesinger & Parisi [2004] for a review of connectionist models in development).

Two important points need to be made here: First, our model does not have mechanisms devoted to processing specific kinds of information, and does not perform explicit hypothesis testing (c.f. Bayesian approaches to modeling cognition). Our claim is not that the model presented here is the only way in which learning about static and dynamic properties can occur. Nonetheless, the model illustrates that it is possible to account for the formation of object concepts in infancy that incorporate static and dynamic features without relying on domain-specific mechanisms, without initial "knowledge," and without explicit hypothesis-testing.

Second, the model operates only on *perceptual* relations. We believe that learning about the motion properties of objects as they move across time and space and as they play different roles in different events do not require domain-specific or theory-driven knowledge (see also Jones & Smith, 1993; Quinn & Eimas, 1997). However, missing from the present account is an exploration of the likely rich role played by context and real-world constraints in the formation of such concepts. Infants undoubtedly notice not only that birds fly but also that this flying event generally occurs outdoors, that lights turn on at night and colors are harder to see in the dark, that heavier objects make louder sounds when they fall—information present in the environment that is all too easy to take for granted. And yet such

31

relations constitute real sources of information that a general-purpose associative learning device such as a connectionist network can integrate into conceptual representations (Clark, 1997). Crucially, such object concepts need not have explicit representations of any of the features that contributed to their formation. For instance, the concept of *bird* need not have an explicit representation of a feature such as *flies_outdoors*. Such knowledge is represented in a connectionist architecture in the strength of inter- and intra-concept connections (i.e., associations).

Embedded within the framework of connectionism is the second feature of the theory: the notion that development is a continuous process. In the model, the apparent discontinuities in learning and behavior emerge not from activation of specific mechanisms or modules, but rather due to nonlinear properties basic to the architecture. The idea that qualitative change in performance is possible through gradual, quantitative changes in representations is something often neglected in developmental accounts (e.g., Gelman, 1990; Mandler, 1992; Piaget, 1952). Even when investigators are sensitive to this possibility, the way in which such gradual changes produce different behaviors is generally unspecified. For instance, Younger and Cohen (1986), observed that while 7-month-old infants were sensitive to correlations between static features of an object, 4-month-old infants were only encoding the individual features. The authors were agnostic as to what accounted for this pattern of behavior. Several recent computational models of Younger and Cohen's (1986) experiments demonstrated that the qualitative change from encoding specific features to correlations among features is easily modeled by a single mechanism exhibiting continuous development (Gureckis & Love, 2004; Westermann & Mareschal, 2004). No separate mechanisms for encoding specific kinds of features and correlations among those features needed to be assumed.

The third feature of our theory concerns inherent learning biases. We assume that not all features in the environment command the same level of attention. In particular, infants are known to attend preferentially to moving stimuli (Slater, 1989). This attentional bias is implemented in the model as a parameter that makes moving aspects of the stimuli more salient to the network (see below for more details). As we outlined earlier, preferential attention to motion does not necessarily imply an ability to fully encode that motion. Moving stimuli, while commanding more attention, are also more difficult to encode accurately due to their continuously changing state.

The fourth feature of the theory is that sensitivity to correlations among certain features—that is, between static and dynamic features and between multiple dynamic features—emerges due to the correlational structure that exists within the categories to which infants are exposed. We modeled the input patterns presented to the network after stimuli used to test infants in previous work (Rakison, 2004, 2005a, 2006; Rakison & Poulin-Dubois,

2002), which themselves were assumed to be consistent with those in the real world. This makes it possible to determine whether there are sufficient statistical regularities in the input for networks to extract the same types of correlations as infants. Before being "habituated" the networks were also trained on corpora of items that embody presumed real-world relations such as the correlation between being an agent of a causal action and possessing dynamic parts (Rakison, 2005a).

Although development is modeled as a continuous process, we recognize that advances in concept formation are determined in large part by improvements in information-processing abilities and neural maturation—presented as the fifth feature of our framework. To model this process, older infants were represented by networks that not only have greater prior experience but also have greater memory and consolidation abilities (see below for implementation details).

Finally, in line with the sixth feature of our theory, the model is able to show how constraints on learning can emerge based on expectations derived from previous experience. The networks used to model performance of older infants were given more experience with encoding correlations between various features that are typical of those found in the real world. We show how this prior experience with real-world correlations produces constraints on learning relations inconsistent with those in the real world. We test this hypothesis in the context of learning of the relation between different object parts and an object's causal role or its ability to self-propel in simple causal and noncausal events.

A DISCUSSION OF PARAMETERS AND ASSUMPTIONS

Most models depend on parameters, and the current model is no exception. In instantiating the assumptions of CAAL, we needed to assign numerical values to many parameters: for example, the strength of perceptual biases for static and dynamic features, the length of habituation, and the amount of prior experience at various age-groups. We also needed to make assumptions with regard to representing the input to which the model was exposed: for example, how many input units would there be and how many time-steps per learning trial. Whenever possible, we turned to the empirical studies for guidance. For instance, both the models and the infants observed three repetitions of each event per learning trial, and we tried to design the inputs to be roughly similar to the inputs used in the empirical studies that we model (see Figure 4). However, a straightforward translation from infant to neural network is rarely possible (after all, we make no claim that the neural networks are full cognitive models of the human cognitive apparatus). For instance, it is not clear how to translate the

33

number of time-steps in a learning trial to a behavioral measure. It is equally unclear whether such a translation would be at all meaningful. It is therefore important to distinguish theoretically important parameters—those involved in implementing the features of CAAL—from arbitrary parameters, for instance, the exact number of habituation trials, or the momentum parameter of the backpropagation algorithm. We present the parameter values that are central to the theoretical account as values in Tables 2, 6, and 7. The more arbitrary parameters are reproduced in "Methods" for completeness rather than theoretical relevance.

A common criticism of computational models is that they can be made to account for any findings by tweaking different parameters. If so, a mere fit to data cannot be used as support of the theory the implemented by the model (e.g., Roberts & Pashler, 2000). This criticism is particularly apt if the model's only claim is fitting existing data and if the parameters have to be tweaked to account for each experimental finding. Our solution to the parameter-setting dilemma was threefold. First, we start out with a set of parameters in Simulation 1 that are then used with minimal modifications for the remaining simulations. Second, we make some novel predictions with existing parameters which are then tested empirically. Third, we make several attempts to demonstrate the robustness of the reported results by examining the impact of varying the theoretically relevant parameters to examine the degree to which the results we report depend on the selection of particular parameters.

SIMULATIONS

In the chapters that follow we provide a computational account of CAAL. Simulations 1a, 1b, and 1c model a series of experiments with 10–18-month-old infants (Rakison & Poulin-Dubois, 2002) that examined the role of moving parts in the emergence of sensitivity to correlations between object properties. We show that motion can act as a facilitatory cue to learning correlations between dynamic features of a stimulus. Simulations 2a and 2b extend the model to the learning of categories, showing that as with infants (Rakison, 2004), learning correlations between dynamic features is more difficult in a category context. In Simulation 3, we use the networks developed in the earlier simulations to test a novel prediction regarding the effects of verbal labels on the encoding of correlated motion cues. The simulation makes a novel prediction regarding which features of a stimulus infants are likely to correlate with concurrently presented labels. Experiments 1a and 1b present empirical work with 18-month-old infants that tests the predictions made by the model.

34

Simulations 4 and 5 examine more closely the emergence of constraints on learning based on prior experience. We show that previous experience encoding particular relations can constrain learning in the domains of causal (Simulation 4) and noncausal (Simulation 5) motion in which agent–recipient relations and self-propulsion are observed. The simulations show a learning trajectory from being insensitive to a particular relation such as whether agents should have moving or static parts, to encoding equally relations both consistent and inconsistent with those in the real world, to displaying a bias for learning about new objects consistent with prior experience, such as the tendency for agents to have moving parts. This pattern of learning is precisely what is observed in infants when tested on these types of relations (Rakison, 2005a, 2006).

NOTE

3. For instance, when presented with items that cluster into several perceptual categories, an auto-associator will tend to extract the dimensions that most are important for representing the broadest distinctions between the items—shown to be equivalent to principal components analysis or singular-value decomposition statistical techniques (Baldi & Hornik, 1989; but see Japkowicz, Hanson, & Gluck, 2000).

III. SIMULATIONS 1a, 1b, AND 1c: THE ROLE OF MOVING PARTS IN FORMING REPRESENTATIONS OF OBJECTS

The aim of the first series of simulations was to show that a domain-general associative learning mechanism tends to show a progression of sensitivity to correlations between static and dynamic parts similar to that of infants. An additional goal was to show that early in development, motion can act as a facilitatory cue to encoding correlations.

Rakison and Poulin-Dubois (2002) used a novel version of the Switch design to examine how infants learn the identity of objects that travel along distinct motion paths. Infants at 10, 14, and 18 months of age were presented with two motion events in which an object moved across a screen. Each object had of a distinct body (red oval shape or blue pot shape), a pair of distinct moving parts (yellow cigar shapes that moved horizontally or green diamond shapes that moved vertically), and a distinct motion path (rectilinear or curvilinear). The stimuli and motion paths used by Rakison and Poulin-Dubois (2002) are presented in Figure 3. Thus, during habituation infants saw, for example, a blue-bodied object with yellow horizontally moving parts travel along a linear trajectory and a red-bodied object with green vertically moving parts travel along a curvilinear trajectory.

There were four test events following habituation. Infants were presented with one event in which the parts were switched in relation to the pairing seen during habituation (parts switch), one event in which the body was switched in relation to the pairing seen during habituation (body switch), one event in which the motion was switched compared with that seen earlier (motion switch), and one event that was the same as that presented in habituation (familiar). The aim of this design was to establish to the developmental trajectory for which features or correlations among the features infants attended when presented with moving, dynamic stimuli. That is, based on the events to which infants dishabituated relative to the familiar event it was possible to determine which correlations they had encoded during the habituation phase. Table 4 highlights the correlations that were violated during each of the test trials.

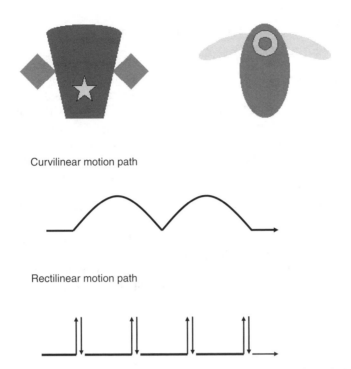

Curvilinear motion path

Rectilinear motion path

FIGURE 3.—Stimuli and motion paths used in Rakison and Poulin-Dubois (2002). *Note.*—Reprinted from *Child Development, 13*, David H. Rakison and Diane Poulin-Dubois, You go this way and I'll go that way: Developmental changes in infants' detection of correlations among static and dynamic features of motion events, pp. 682–699, Copyright (2002), permission from Wiley-Blackwell Publishing Ltd.

The results of the experiment revealed that infants at 10 months of age failed to learn any of the correlations in the events, and a subsequent simulation revealed that they encoded only the static bodies of the objects and not the dynamic parts or motion trajectory of the objects. In contrast, infants at 14 months encoded only the relation between object parts and the motion trajectory of an object (curvilinear or rectilinear); that is, they dishabituated only to the parts-switch event relative to the familiar event. Moreover, a follow-up experiment showed that they did so only when the parts of the object moved. Finally, infants at 18 months encoded all of the correlations available in the events—they looked longer at all three switch events than the familiar event—and they encoded only the relation between parts and motion trajectory when the parts did not move. Note that these empirical studies did not examine specifically whether constraints on learning emerge as a product of prior experience with statistical regularities; that is, infants older than 22 months of age were not tested with stimuli that were inconsistent with those found in the real world (see, e.g., Rakison, 2005a, 2006) and the curvilinear and rectilinear motion paths were not representative of how things move in the world (compared with the causal events and self-propulsion tested by Rakison, 2005a, 2006). Consequently, this developmental pattern will not be explored in the simulations in this chapter.

Simulation 1a modeled the performance of 14-month-olds, comparing the correlations learned by the network when presented with moving parts versus static parts. Simulation 1b repeated this for 18-month-olds. Simulation 1c tested the model's ability to predict performance of younger infants. Younger and Cohen (1986) found that infants as young as 4 months were capable of encoding individual static features, yet older infants may be incapable of encoding dynamic features because it is more difficult to encode moving stimuli despite their attention-grabbing nature (Rakison & Poulin-Dubois, 2002). In support for this contention Rakison and Poulin-Dubois (2002, Experiment 4) demonstrated that when 10-month-olds were habituated on a single stimulus with moving parts, the infants dishabituated only to a novel body and failed to encode any dynamic features of the stimulus. Simulation 1c tested the model's ability to account for this result.

METHOD

Network Architecture

We used a simple recurrent network (Elman, 1990) that was trained using a variant of standard backpropagation with momentum (Doug's Momentum: http://tedlab.mit.edu/ ~ dr/Lens/Commands/dougsMomentum. html). The input consisted of patterns of activity across three groups of units, corresponding to the body, parts, and global motion of the stimuli used by Rakison and Poulin-Dubois (2002; see Figure 3). The input layer projected to two groups of hidden units through fast-learning (FL) and slow-learning (SL) connections (see Figure 4). The FL connections had high learning rates ($\alpha = 0.2$), but also high weight-decay (see Table 3). The SL connections had lower learning rate ($\alpha = 0.001$), and low weight-decay (0.0001).

The rationale for incorporating these FL and SL connections in the network was that it allowed us to assess the role of previous experience on the network (Hinton & Plaut, 1987). Standard three-layer networks are subject to a phenomenon called *catastrophic interference* (e.g., McCloskey & Cohen, 1989). Unless old and new training patterns are interleaved during training, new material tends to overwrite what was previously learned because both make use of the same connections. Using FL and SL connections is one way in which a network can be exposed to background information that can then influence on-line performance during and after subsequent training. Although there are a number of potential solutions for avoiding catastrophic interference we chose to implement FL and SL connections because the

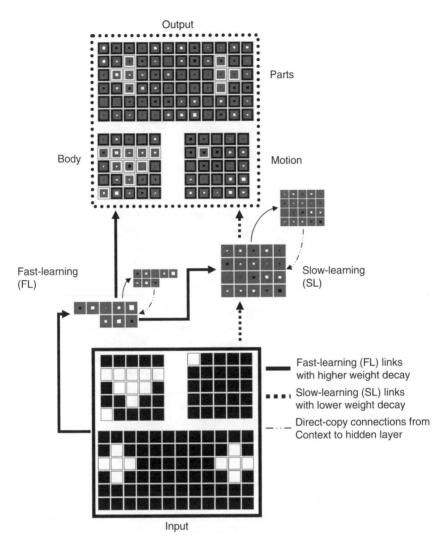

FIGURE 4.—The architecture of the network. Input groups are fully connected to the two hidden layers, which are in turn fully and symmetrically connected to the output layers. White-filled squares indicate units fully active (have a value of 1), black squares indicate units turned off (a value of 0). White outlines indicate a target value of 1, black outlines indicate a target value of 0.

interplay between them is neurologically plausible to some extent, corresponding to a simple implementation of hippocampus–cortical complimentary learning systems (McClelland, McNaughton, & O'Reilly, 1995).

Development in the networks was modeled by altering the number of hidden units in the FL hidden layer and by altering the weight-decay

TABLE 3

PARAMETERS USED IN SIMULATIONS 1–3

Age (months)	Hidden Units (FL/SL)	Pretraining Epochs	Habituation Epochs	Weight Decay
10	5/20	10	30	0.05
14	8/20	50	30	0.01
18	10/20	200	30	0.001
22	14/20	300	30	0.0005

Note.—FL, fast learning; SL, slow learning.

parameter of the FL links with "older" networks having more FL hidden units and a lower weight-decay in the FL links. Increasing the number of hidden units allows a network both to store more information, as well as to be more sensitive to the details of the training set. Decreasing the weight-decay corresponds to a more robust interaction between the SL and FL units, allowing the network to extract both more information from the habituation stimuli, and integrate the information with previously learned relations. Together, the two parameters implement a very simple model of neural maturation of working memory. Although it may be reasonable to map the FL and SL layers to the hippocampus and cortex, respectively, we wish to avoid making this link. Rather, we assume that the neural architecture of infant brains has mechanisms for learning new information while retaining what was previously learned. We further assumed that this ability improves with age—using FL and SL units with weight-decay that decreases with age is an implementation of this assumption.

There are several possible shortcomings to the way we implemented development in the model. Clearly it is a simplification to simulate development only in terms of these two parameters. However, keeping other parameters constant allowed for parsimony—modeling development in terms of a few well-understood parameters. We also recognize that because manipulations of the number of hidden units and decreasing weight-decay are occurring independent of experience, it does not constitute true experience-dependent learning (Munakata & McClelland, 2003; Johnson & Munakata, 2005) (see Experience-Dependent Learning in the General Discussion for more on this issue), and hence our account of development relies on maturation to some degree (for discussion, see Quinn et al., 2000). However, in addition to architectural differences between networks used to model infants of different ages, we also varied the amount of prior experience given to the various networks: "Older" networks were exposed to a greater number of "pretraining" trials embodying correlations present in the world (see Table 3 for a listing of the parameters used for the different ages). This component of the implementation of development is fully compatible with experience-dependent frameworks. By being exposed to a greater proportion of correlations consistent with real-world relations than correlations inconsistent with the real world, the networks become biased to learning the former, with older networks being less able to learn inconsistent relations despite having more powerful computational resources (see Simulations 4–5).

A network biased through experience in such a way can be described to have certain priors (e.g., expecting agents to have moving parts). Although we use the word "prior" to denote a concept in some ways similar to a prior in a Bayesian framework (e.g., Tenenbaum, Griffiths, & Kemp, 2006), our notion of priors is qualitatively different from Bayesian priors in two ways. First, in the present model there is no explicit representation of the bias (prior). The bias is distributed through the same connections that process the incoming information. A second, related point is that while in a Bayesian approach the priors are set ahead of time, in our model they arise gradually as the network accumulates information from multiple examples during the pretraining stage.

Feature three of the CAAL framework concerned innate attentional biases, specifically infants' preference to attend to dynamic over static stimuli (Rakison & Poulin-Dubois, 2002; Slater, 1989). In the model, attentional biases were modeled as a scaling parameter that controlled the output error. When the parts were moving, the values 1, 5, and 10 were used for the body, moving parts, and global motion, respectively. When the parts were not moving, we assumed that infants would pay less attention to the parts, but more attention to the global motion. For the simulations with no moving parts, the values 1, 1, and 15 were used for the body, static parts, and global motion, respectively. (Note that although these values were somewhat arbitrary, we will demonstrate that using different values does not change the results of the simulation.) This implementation creates a "pool" of attention that is spread across the different features of a stimulus. The direct effect of this scaling was to make groups with larger attentional parameters more salient during training.

It is important to point out that salience does not automatically result in better learning, merely that the process of error minimization is more dominated by the group with the largest attentional parameter. A consequence of modeling attention in this way is that a network incapable of encoding a feature—such as complex motion—may nevertheless attempt to encode this feature at the expense of encoding features that it would otherwise be able to learn. The architecture therefore enabled us to investigate the somewhat paradoxical status of motion in object concepts. On the one hand, motion attracts attention (Kanazawa, Shira, Ohtsuka, & Yamaguchi, 2006; Slater, 1989), but on the other hand, the motion itself can be difficult to encode for young infants (Rakison, 2005a; Rakison & Poulin-Dubois, 2002; Shira, Kanazawa, & Yamaguchi, 2006).

Materials

The stimuli and training were modeled after the switch design procedure used by Rakison and Poulin-Dubois (2002). The training corpus contained two stimuli. Each stimulus had associated with it a distinct body, a distinct motion trajectory, and distinct parts that were either static or moved in a cyclical pattern (see Appendix A). The shapes and motions of the stimuli roughly corresponded to the shapes and motions used by Rakison and Poulin-Dubois (2002; see Figure 3) due to our assumption that infants, like networks, are sensitive to perceptual overlap in the habituation stimuli (Figure 5). In addition to the habituation stimuli, we generated additional stimuli used for pretraining. These stimuli had different bodies, parts, and global motions from the stimuli used in habituation (see "Training" for more details).

There are several potential criticisms concerning the design of the training items. First, the parts, body, and global motion layers had different numbers of units. This is not a serious concern because the error used in the computations is normalized for each layer, thereby taking into account the different number of units. In other words, although the motion layer contained only one unit, its contribution is equivalent to the parts and body layers that contained many more units (see "Testing"). Second, we recognize that the division of the input array into parts, body, and global motion layers and conflating local motion with parts is somewhat arbitrary. Alternative implementations, for instance, may have combined the global motion and body layers, and separated the local motion and parts layers. Nonetheless, we have no reason to suspect that such architectural distinctions

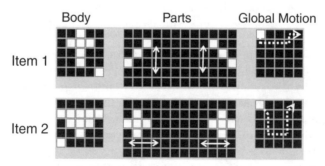

FIGURE 5.—The two training patterns used in Experiments 1a and b. The white arrows indicate the motion trajectory which cycles every three time steps for the parts and every seven time steps for the global motion.

would qualitatively alter the results or would be better motivated by the theory we presented here. From the perspective of the network, there is nothing labeling the parts layer as "parts" and the body layer as "body." The identity of these layers is determined by the pattern of correlations present in the input. A shortcoming of the current implementation that is potentially relevant is the separation of the global motion and body layers, which results in the activity in the body layer beings constant for the duration of the trial while, in reality, the body undergoes the global motion pattern. This separation would not be necessary if our model more accurately implemented the physiology of the human visual system (e.g., separating the object identity and location into separate streams [Ungerleider & Mishkin, 1982]). However, such a level of detail was beyond the scope of the present model. To capture object constancy—that body$_a$ remains body$_a$ even when it is in a different part of the visual field—we found it necessary to separate the body identity and the body motion into two layers (see Földiák, 1998, for computational approaches to object constancy). Because parts and the motion of the parts were always perfectly correlated, the two were conflated into the same layer. Separating parts into a static parts layer and dynamic part–motion layer did not qualitatively alter the results.

Procedure

On each time step, information from the input array created a pattern of activity in the hidden and output layers. On each subsequent time step, the pattern of activation was copied into context-layers, which then fed back onto the hidden layers, providing the network with a simple short-term memory. The network's output was therefore based not only on the current input pattern, but also on its activity from the previous input. The task of the network at time t was to predict what happened at time $t+1$ by turning on the appropriate units in the output layer. Because static patterns remained the same from one time step to another, the network could learn static patterns through simple auto-association. For dynamic parts of the array, namely the global motion and moving parts, the network needed to predict the next time step using both the current activation and the context. Learning consisted of minimizing the error between the predicted and observed outputs. Each event thus consisted of a series of frames and given a particular frame, the network's goal was to predict the next frame. See Appendix A for an illustration of the series of frames. After the end of each event, all units were reset to their default state of 0.

Although the input separates features corresponding to the body, parts, and motion of the stimulus into separate input layers, all the input layers are connected to the same set of hidden units. The hidden layer can, in principle, encode isolated features of the stimulus, but it can also encode

43

correlations between the features. The degree to which correlations are learned will be shown to depend on the structure of the training set and the training and attentional parameters used. Crucial to the present account is that the same units and links in the hidden layer are responsible for learning the representation of all the features of the input array. Although the input and output layers separate the stimulus into discrete aspects (body, motion, and parts), the network must represent the stimulus using the same set of weights, and so needs to recombine the information from all input layers. The degree to which correlations are represented depends on how the information is recombined.

Training

After being initialized with small random weights, networks underwent two stages of training: "pretraining" and "habituation." The first stage corresponded to "real-world" experience of the infant coming into the experiment. During this stage, the networks were trained on a corpus of eight patterns embodying several regularities: (1) part motions were always correlated with global motions, (2) static parts were not correlated with global motions,[4] (3) bodies were correlated with global motions with a probability of 2/3. During pretraining, all the network weights (both FL and SL links) were free to change. The second stage corresponded to the habituation condition and was modeled after the procedure used in Rakison and Poulin-Dubois (2002). During habituation training, the FL weights were free to change and the SL weights were fixed. The rationale for this procedure was that although habituation can produce relatively long-term memories lasting a day or even a week (for a review, see Rovee-Collier & Gerhardstein, 1997), it is unlikely that previous knowledge brought to the laboratory would be significantly altered by a brief period of repeated presentations of a set of stimuli. To be clear, we are not implying that infants in habituation experiments learn any differently than they do in the real world; instead, we suggest that learning that leads to durable representations lasting longer than hours or days is slow and requires many more training trials—or put simply experience—than that available in habituation.

Each training trial consisted of seven time steps repeated three times (see Appendix A). The three repetitions of the events corresponded to the number of times that animated scenes were shown to infants in various studies by Rakison (Rakison & Poulin-Dubois, 2002; Rakison, 2004, 2005a, 2006). Weights were updated after each pass through the corpus. After training, the network's learning was assessed by testing it on "switch trials"—stimuli in which some correlations are broken, and some preserved, again modeled after Rakison and Poulin-Dubois (2002). The pattern of "dishabituation" provides insight into the correlations learned by the network.

Testing

Following training, the network's learning was assessed by testing it on patterns that violated correlations between the features of the stimuli. To measure the sensitivity of the network to these correlations, the network's error when presented with a switch trial was compared with its error when presented with a familiar trial. The most common interpretation of visual dishabituation in infants is that it indicates a discrepancy between the representation, or neural or mental model, that is generated during habituation and the perceptual input that is presented following habitation (see, e.g., Gilmore & Thomas, 2002). Similarly, larger errors in a network indicate a discrepancy between what is observed (the pattern of activity across the output layer), and what is expected (the target information in the output layer which is derived from the input layer). As in Rakison and Poulin-Dubois (2002), there were four test trials (see Table 4). In one test trial, the *parts switch*, the parts from one object were presented with the motion and body of the other object presented during habituation. In a second test trial, the *body switch*, the body from one object was presented with the motion and parts of the other object presented during habituation. In a third test trial, the *motion switch*, the motion of one object was presented with the body and parts of the other object presented during habituation. The fourth test trial, the *familiar test*, was identical to that presented during habituation.

TABLE 4

SWITCH TRIALS USED IN SIMULATIONS 1A AND B

Example	Body	Global Motion	Parts	Correlations Unchanged	Correlations Violated
Habituation trials					
Trial 1	Red	Rectilinear	Green		
Trial 2	Blue	Curvilinear	Yellow		
Test trials					
Parts switch	Red	Rectilinear	Yellow	Body–motion	Parts–body Parts–motion
Body switch	Blue	Rectilinear	Green	Parts–motion	Parts–body Body–motion
Motion switch	Blue	Rectilinear	Yellow	Parts–body	Parts–motion Body–motion
Familiar	Red	Rectilinear	Green	Parts–body–motion	None

45

We used network error as a measure of "looking time" (Mareschal, 2003; Sirois & Mareschal, 2002). Because the output layers were of different sizes we could not simply combine the error from each of the three output layers. Instead, the error for a particular test pattern was expressed as a ratio of the current error divided by the average error from each layer produced by an untrained network. The overall error was calculated using the following formula:

$$TotalError = \left(\frac{ErrorBody}{UntrainedErrorBody} \right) + \left(\frac{ErrorParts}{UntrainedErrorParts} \right) + \left(\frac{ErrorMotion}{UntrainedErrorMotion} \right) \tag{1}$$

The error scores were then standardized by dividing the product by the mean of the familiar stimulus so that the familiar-test trials always had a mean of 1. While network error directly reflects the mismatch between a network's output (prediction) and the test item, infant looking times are only indirect measures of the discrepancy between mental representation of a stimulus and what is observed during a test trial (Sirois & Mareschal, 2002). Although it was not the goal of the present model to account for individual differences, we felt it important to produce some degree of inter-trial variability so characteristic of human data (Cohen & Menten, 1981). This was achieved by adding a small amount of noise to the network error: Normal distribution, $M = 0$; $SD = 0.01$.

The degree of "dishabituation" to a switch trial was the difference between the normalized familiar stimulus and switch trials. By the logic of the switch design, a difference between a familiar and a switch trial reflects sensitivity to a particular correlation (Younger & Cohen, 1986). For instance, a difference between the familiar and the parts switch indicates that the network was sensitive to the parts–body and/or parts–motion correlations.

In addition to comparing the aggregate errors of the familiar- and switch-test trials, we also examined the difference between the network's hidden unit activity to the familiar- and switch-test trials after habituation. If training the network on stimuli with moving parts results in stronger correlations between the dynamic properties of the stimulus, then this should be reflected in a greater difference in representations (hidden unit activity) between the familiar and switch trials. To perform this analysis, we computed the Euclidean distances between the activations of the units in the FL hidden layer when the network was tested on a familiar trial, and when tested on one of the three switch trials. We then compared these representational distances in the moving-parts condition to the static-parts condition.

46

RESULTS

For each of the simulations presented here, the data were averaged across 10 separate runs with networks initialized with small random weights. The results were analyzed using a repeated-measures ANOVA with test trial as a fixed factor and network as a random factor. Planned comparisons of switch trials with the familiar condition were performed using the Bonferroni simultaneous tests. For simplicity, we will refer to the models of various age groups as "14-month-old networks," "16-month-old networks," and so on. The models presented here should not be taken as cognitive architectures of infants of the corresponding ages but rather a way to implement specific tasks in a model that embodies domain-general associative learning and the other assumptions of the CAAL framework described above. Also note that here and throughout the manuscript it is the developmental pattern of the networks at different "ages" that is important and not whether we were able to model the behaviors of specific age groups of infants in networks of the same "age."

Simulation 1a

Figure 6 shows errors (averaged across 10 networks) from the three output layers over the course of habituation for the moving-parts and static-parts conditions. For the purposes of the figure, the errors from the three layers were normalized to 1 at the start of training; the *y*-axis therefore records the proportional decrease of the error in each layer with respect to the starting error which compensates for the different number of units in the body, parts, and global motion layers.

The two conditions—moving parts and static parts—differed on the attentional parameter in the parts group. Under the assumption that infants are attracted to motion, moving parts were made more salient to the network during habituation by scaling the output error and derivatives of the parts layer. We also reasoned that paying attention to moving parts would draw attention away from the global motion of the stimulus; consequently, the motion was made less salient in the moving-parts condition compared with the static-parts condition. Figure 6 shows that networks exposed to static parts exhibited a faster decrease in habituation error for the global motion layer than networks habituated to moving parts: paired *t*-test comparing prediction errors from the global motion layer, $t(29) = 7.37$, $p < .0005$. The pattern was reversed in the parts layer: The greater "attention" placed on moving parts resulted in faster learning of the parts, $t(29) = 6.87$, $p < .0005$. Most interesting is the right-most panel of Figure 6 that shows habituation performance on the body layer. The bodies of the moving- and static-parts stimuli were exactly the same, as were all the

47

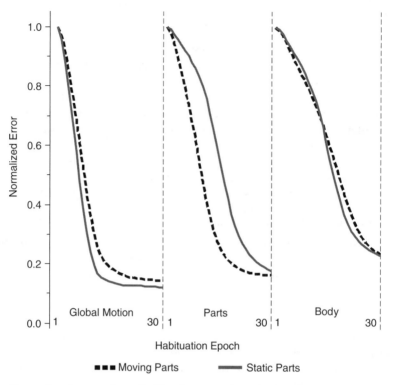

FIGURE 6.—A comparison of habituation errors from the three layers in Experiment 1a when parts are static (solid line) and when parts are moving (dashed line).

learning parameters. Nevertheless, networks habituated to moving parts learned the information in the body layer slightly slower than networks habituated to static parts, $t(29) = 2.27$, $p < .05$. Notice, however, that in the first half of the habituation period, the moving-parts condition actually produced a *smaller* error in the body layer than the static-parts condition. Overall it appears that the moving parts initially act as facilitatory cues to learning the body, but the greater attention devoted to the moving parts makes it on the whole more difficult to learn this static feature. As predicted, the global motion was more difficult to learn than the moving parts, resulting in an overall greater error during habituation (this was true despite more attentional weight being placed on the motion than the moving parts), paired t-test of raw errors controlled for number of units in the output layers: $t(29) = 5.77$, $p < .0005$.

After habituation, we analyzed the performance of the networks on the familiar and switch trials. Analysis of the 14-month-old networks that were habituated to stimuli with moving parts revealed a significant effect of test

48

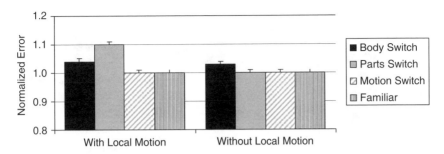

FIGURE 7.—Simulation 1a: (Rakison & Poulin Dubois, 2002; Experiment 1). Networks simulating 14-month-old infants trained on moving, but not static parts dishabituate to a parts switch, indicating that moving parts help to encode the correlation between the parts and the body and/or motion.

trial, $F(3, 27) = 20.84$, $p < .0005$. The performance of the networks on the familiar- and switch-test trials are presented in Figure 7. Planned comparisons revealed a significant difference between the familiar stimulus and the parts-switch trial, $t(9) = 6.96$, $p < .0005$. No other comparisons were significant. Identical networks habituated to stimuli with static parts (Figure 7) showed no reliable differences between the familiar and switch trials, $F(3, 27) < 1$, NS, all t's < 1.

The exact results reported in the present simulations do depend on the parameter values chosen. However, the overall patterns of results hold for a range of parameter values rather than depending on precise values. As a demonstration of this point, we re-ran Simulation 1a after making the following changes to the parameters from those listed in Table 3: The FL weight-decay was changed to 0.025, the number of habituation trials was changed to 50, and the attentional parameters were changed from 1, 5, and 10, to 0.5, 1, and 2 for the body, moving parts, and global motion, respectively. Despite these changes, the pattern found in Simulation 1a still held: the networks habituated to stimuli with moving parts dishabituated to the parts-switch trial—overall $F(3, 27) = 11.17$, $p < .0005$ with only the parts switch significantly different from the familiar-test trial: $t(9) = 4.58$, $p < .001$. When the parts were static, there was no overall effect of test trial: $F(3, 27) = 2.27$, $p > .1$. The parts-switch and familiar-test trials now yielded errors that were not significantly different, $t(9) = 1.09$.

To analyze further the representations of the network, we used the hidden unit activations in the FL hidden layer to compute Euclidean distances between the activations to the familiar and each of the switch trials and compared these distances for the moving-parts and static-parts conditions. This analysis revealed a significant difference between the conditions only for the parts-switch trial: paired t-test comparing Euclidean distances on each time step: $t(6) = 3.16$, $p < .02$. Habituation to the stimuli

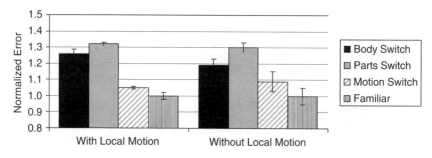

FIGURE 8.—Simulation 1b: (Rakison & Poulin Dubois, 2002; Experiment 2). Moving parts facilitate encoding of correlations for simulated 18-month-old infants.

with moving parts did not produce greater differentiation between the familiar- and motion-switch trials, $t(6) < 1$, or the familiar- and body-switch trials, $t(6) = 1.81, p > .1$.

Simulation 1b

More sophisticated 18-month-old networks habituated on the moving parts showed a significant effect of test trial, $F(3, 27) = 91.79$, $p < .0005$. There were significant differences between the familiar trial and the body switch: $t(9) = 11.48, p < .0005$, the parts switch, $t(9) = 13.82, p < .0005$, and a smaller, but reliable difference between the familiar- and the motion-switch trial, $t(9) = 2.23, p < .05$. For the networks pretrained and habituated with static parts (see Figure 8), there was also a significant effect of test trial, $F(3, 27) = 7.45, p < .005$. There was a highly reliable difference between the familiar- and the parts-switch trial, $t(9) = 4.53, p < .001$, a reliable effect for the body-switch trial, $t(9) = 2.53, p < .03$ and no reliable difference between the familiar- and motion-switch trials, $t(9) = 1.29, p > .3$ (see Figure 8).

Comparisons Between Simulations 1a and 1b

To demonstrate further the effects of moving parts on the 14- and 18-month-old networks, we performed cross-simulation ANOVAs. We found a marginally significant three-way interaction between age, test trial (parts, body, or motion switch), and motion condition (static or moving parts), $F(2, 18) = 2.89, p = .06$. Restricting the analysis to just the parts trial, there was a significant interaction between the condition (with or without motion), and age (14 or 18 months), $F(1, 18) = 10.98, p < .005$, indicating that the moving parts had an effect on the parts-switch trial for simpler 14-month-old networks but not the more sophisticated 18-month-old networks.

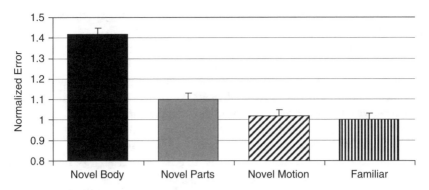

FIGURE 9.—Simulation 1c: (Rakison & Poulin-Dubois, 2002; Experiment 4). Network modeling 10-month-old infants trained on one stimulus with a moving part dishabituate most to the object body.

Simulation 1c

To assess whether "younger" networks could discriminate the individual features of the stimuli (see Rakison & Poulin-Dubois, 2002), 10-month-old networks were habituated to a single stimulus with moving parts. The results revealed a significant effect of test trial, $F(3, 27) = 65.18$, $p < .001$, which was mostly driven by the novel body trial, $t(9) = 12.19$, $p < .0005$. As can be seen in Figure 9, there was also a significant increase in error for the novel parts trial $t(9) = 2.52$, $p < .03$; however, this increase was much smaller than the one for the novel body, $t(9) = 9.67$, $p < .0005$. There was no increase in error for the novel motion trial, $t(9) < 1$.

DISCUSSION

Results from Simulation 1a precisely matched the developmental pattern observed in Experiment 1 of Rakison and Poulin-Dubois (2002): The network and 14-month-old infants dishabituated to the parts-switch trial only when presented with objects that possessed moving parts during habitation, indicating that moving parts facilitated the learning of the parts–body and/or parts–global motion correlations. In addition to using aggregate errors as a measure of dishabituation, we confirmed the effect through analysis of the representations of the hidden-units, showing that the difference in representations between the familiar- and parts-switch trial is greater in the moving-parts condition than in the static-parts condition. Besides aiding the learning of correlations, the presence of moving parts alters the learning of the individual "features" of the stimuli, as can be seen in Figure 6. The differences between learning the motion and parts can be explained by the differences in attention between the moving- and static-parts conditions yet the difference in learning the body cannot. The presence of

51

moving parts detracted attention away from the body. At the same time, early in habituation the moving parts may act as facilitatory cues to learning the body of the objects.

Simulation 1b results matched the qualitative pattern observed in Experiment 2 of Rakison and Poulin-Dubois's (2002); that is, the networks and 18-month-old infants dishabituated to all the switch trials when habituated to objects with moving parts. In contrast, when habituated to static parts, 18-month-old infants dishabituated only to the parts-switch trial. The networks showed reliable increases in error to both the parts-switch and body-switch trials, but the increase in error to the parts-switch trial was significantly greater than that to the body-switch trials.

In Experiment 4 of Rakison and Poulin-Dubois (2002), the authors tested whether 10-month-olds were able to encode the individual features (parts, body, or motion) presented in the events and found that infants dishabituated to the novel body but not to a novel global motion or novel moving parts. Simulation 1c replicated this pattern. Although the network did show a reliable increase in error to novel parts, it was significantly smaller than the increase in error to the novel body (see Figure 9). Recall that because network errors were normalized with respect to the size of each layer (Equation 1), the different sizes of the layers (Figure 5) have nothing to do with the reported results. That is, although the global motion layer contained only one unit, its small initial error guaranteed that its final contribution was comparable to the parts layer.

The reported pattern of findings suggests that a domain-general associative learning mechanism is sufficient to account for the developmental progression of sensitivity to correlations between static and dynamic features that was observed by Rakison and Poulin-Dubois (2002). The model did not include a motion-specific learning mechanism and there is no evidence that motion was processed differently from any other salient feature(s) in the stimuli. The networks learned that objects with distinct moving parts moved along distinct motion paths and then later, following additional experience and increased information-processing abilities, learned that objects with distinct bodies and moving parts moved along distinct motion trajectories. These findings are striking because although the dynamic features of the stimuli were more difficult to encode—as demonstrated by the 10-month-old infants and networks—they also acted as a facilitatory cue to encoding other correlations.

NOTE

4. We are aware that these correlations are not perfect in the real world. Using imperfect correlations in the pretraining corpus did not alter the qualitative pattern we report here.

IV. SIMULATIONS 2a AND 2b: THE ROLE OF MOVING PARTS IN FORMING REPRESENTATIONS OF OBJECTS PRESENTED IN A CATEGORY CONTEXT

Rakison and Poulin-Dubois (2002) found that 18-month-olds showed sensitivity to all of the presented correlations in the context of two habituation trials; however, Rakison (2004) found that it was not until 22 months that infants were able to encode these correlations in a category context; that is, when they were exposed to four stimuli during habituation trials with some features correlated and other uncorrelated. The aim of this design was to determine whether infants are able to extract correlations shared by two category members in the presence of some level of "noise"—that is, a feature that was not correlated with category membership. In Simulation 2a, the categories presented to the network consisted of correlated moving parts and global motion but uncorrelated bodies. In other words, the categories were defined by correlated parts and global motion and the body was not predictive of either. The design of this study is presented in Table 5.

We predicted that because of the greater information-processing demands inherent in presenting stimuli in a category context, the networks that showed sensitivity to correlations in Simulations 1a and 1b would fail to do so in Simulation 2a. We further predicted that because 22-month-olds in Rakison (2004) showed sensitivity to the part-motion correlation in a category context, a network with more FL units and a lower FL weight-decay than the 18-month-old network would start showing the same sensitivity. Rakison (2004) also showed that infants at 22 months did not encode relations between an object's body and its motion trajectory in a category context. The goal of Simulation 2b was to examine further whether the network was selective in the correlations that it encodes.

METHOD

The procedure for Simulations 2a and 2b was identical to Simulations 1a–1c with several exceptions. Most notably, as in Rakison (2004, Experiment 1) networks corresponding to 14-, 18-, and 22-month-old infants were

TABLE 5

HABITUATION AND TEST STIMULI USED IN SIMULATION 2A REPRESENTED IN
ABSTRACT NOTATION

	Parts	Motion	Body
Habituation stimuli			
	1	1	1
	1	1	2
	2	2	1
	2	2	2
Test stimuli			
Correlated	1	1	2
Uncorrelated	1	2	1

Note.—Each stimulus event possessed three attributes (parts, body, and motion path) that could take one of the two values. The values for each attribute are represented here as 1s and 2s and were yellow vertically moving parts versus green horizontally moving parts, curvilinear versus rectilinear motion paths, and red curvilinear body versus blue rectilinear body. The test stimuli composed of familiar attributes that either maintained the correlation observed during habituation (correlated stimulus) or violated that correlation (uncorrelated stimulus). Note that the feature values of the actual habituation and test stimuli were counterbalanced across infants (taken from Rakison, 2004).

habituated to four instead of two stimuli. These four stimuli could be grouped into two categories on the basis of a correlation between the moving parts and global motion (Simulation 2a), or the body and the global motion (Simulation 2b). So, in Simulation 2a, the networks were habituated to two categories: In each category, the two dynamic features (parts and motion) were correlated while the static feature (the body) was not predictive of category membership. In Simulation 2b, the global motion was not predictive, requiring the networks to correlate body with moving parts. Simulations 2a and 2b, respectively, match experiments 1 and 3b of Rakison (2004).

Following habituation, there were two test trials: the *correlated trial* (identical to one of the habituation trials), and the *uncorrelated trial* that violated the correlation presented during habituation. (The novel trial, present in the infant studies, was left out because it was found the networks always had much greater error to a testing trial that had all novel features.) The results for the correlated test trials were averages of the two categories presented during habituation. This method was employed because it was observed that on some network runs, the network learned one category better than the other meaning that the error to the familiar stimulus would be different depending on which familiar stimulus was used (this was not observed in Simulations 1a, 1b, or 1c).

In the basic design, the correlated stimulus was also a familiar stimulus, having been seen during habituation. It is therefore possible that a difference in error between the correlated and uncorrelated stimulus could

TABLE 6

Habituation and Test Stimuli Used in the *3-Habituation-Stimuli* Condition of Simulation 2a Represented in Abstract Notation

	Parts	Motion	Body
Habituation stimuli			
	1	1	1
	1	1	2
	2	2	1
Test stimuli			
Correlated (but novel)	2	2	2
Uncorrelated	1	2	1

Note.—Now both test stimuli are not included among the habituation stimuli.

therefore be produced by a difference in familiarity. Rakison (2004) tested this possibility by removing the correlated test item from habituation, leaving three habituation trials (Experiment 4). We replicated this in the *3-habituation-stimuli* condition of Simulation 2a. The design of habituation and test trials is depicted in Table 6. Notice that it is identical to the original design (Table 5) except now neither the correlated nor the uncorrelated test items were presented during habituation.

RESULTS

Simulation 2a

As can be seen in Figure 10, neither the 14-month-old nor the 18-month-old networks showed increased error to the uncorrelated test trial in

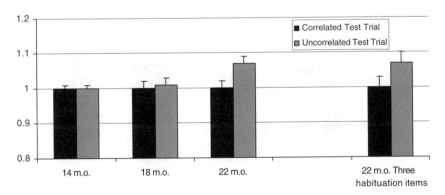

FIGURE 10.—Simulation 2a (Rakison, 2004; Experiment 1): Detecting correlations in a category context—correlated moving parts and global motion.

comparison with the correlated trial: $F(1, 9) < 1$. In contrast, the 22-month-old network showed a reliable increase in error, $F(1, 9) = 7.53, p < .03$, which suggests that it encoded the relation between the parts and motion embedded in a category context. A cross-simulation ANOVA testing the age × testing-trial interaction confirmed this developmental trend from 18 to 22 months, $F(1, 18) = 10.85, p < .005$. The results for the three-habituation-trials condition were very similar (two right-most bars in Figure 10), revealing a significantly greater error in the uncorrelated trials, $F(1, 9) = 7.94, p < .01$. There was no statistical difference between observing the correlated trial during habituation, or not, as measured by cross-simulation ANOVA with habituation-type as a between-network factor and test-trial as a within-network factor, $F(1, 18) = 0.01$, NS.

Simulation 2b

Unlike Simulation 2a, 22-month-old networks showed less sensitivity to the body–motion correlation in a category context (see Figure 11). The difference in error between the correlated and uncorrelated test trials was only marginal, $F(1, 9) = 2.75, p = .13$. The age × test-type interaction with age and test-type as within-subject was marginally significant, $F(1, 18) = 3.84, p = .07$, suggesting that while the networks modeling 22-month-olds were not discriminating the correlated and uncorrelated trials at a significant level, they were performing slightly better than the 18-month-old networks (which were not discriminating the two trials at all).

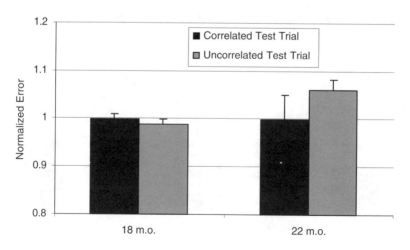

FIGURE 11.—Simulation 2b (Rakison, 2004; Experiment 3a): Detecting correlations in a category context—correlated body and global motion.

TABLE 7

EFFECTS OF CHANGING PARAMETERS FOR SIMULATIONS 2A AND 2B

	Simulation 2a	Simulation 2b
Replication with the original parameters	$F(1,9) = 4.90, p < .05$	$F(1,9) = 3.36, p > .1$
12 hidden units	$F(1,9) = 8.44, p < .01$	$F(1,9) < 1$
0.00025 weight decay	$F(1,9) = 7.14, p < .01$	$F(1,9) = 2.78, p > .1$

The differences between the 22-month old networks in Simulation 2a and 2b were not large and an ANOVA with Simulation (2a, 2b) as a between-network factor and testing type (correlated, uncorrelated) as a within-network factor was not significant $(1, 18) < 1$. However, the effect was robust and was replicable with different parameter values, as discussed below.

In Simulation 2a, but not 2b, the networks modeling the performance of 22-month-old infants dishabituated to the uncorrelated test trial. Because the mean errors of the uncorrelated trials were quite similar in both of the simulations, we re-ran these simulations using a number of different parameters. If the pattern of dishabituation in Simulation 2a but not 2b holds across a range of parameter values, it is additional evidence that the networks have a bias for encoding the parts–motion correlation (Simulation 2a) and the parts–body correlation (Simulation 2b).

We ran three additional simulations, replicating the original simulation, and making the following changes to the parameters (cf, Table 3): (1) The number of hidden units was changed from 14 to 12; (2) the weight-decay was changed from 0.0005 to 0.00025. As before, there were 10 randomly initiated networks run in each simulation. The results are presented in Table 7. As can be seen neither change altered the qualitative pattern we report in the main text.

DISCUSSION

Simulations 2a and 2b tested the model's ability to learn correlations between dynamic features in a category context. The results of the models matched the development trend observed with infants in previous empirical work—although 14-month-old infants were sensitive to the parts–motion correlation when habituated to two stimuli with moving parts (Rakison & Poulin-Dubois, 2002; Experiment 1; and Simulation 1a reported here), it was not until 22 months that the network was able to encode the same correlation in a category context (Rakison, 2004). The claim that the network is displaying a sensitivity to the correlation (rather than, for instance, showing lower error to the correlated trial because it was seen during habituation) is further bolstered by including a condition in which both the correlated and uncorrelated trials were not seen during habituation. The results from this condition were unchanged from the original, with the networks still having greater error to the uncorrelated than correlated trial.

To examine whether the 22-month-old network, like infants in Rakison (2004), was selective in the correlations it would learn, Simulation 2b habituated and tested the network on categories in which the motion path and body were correlated but the parts were not. The results revealed that although the network was sensitive to the parts–motion correlation (Simulation 2a) (as indicated by an increase in error when the correlation was violated), it was less sensitive to the body–motion correlation, mirroring the pattern of the infant data. It is worth reiterating here that the exact age at which this kind of developmental trend is observed in the first years of life may, however, be somewhat different from that found here and in empirical work with infants (Rakison, 2004; Rakison & Poulin-Dubois, 2002).

V. LEARNING INITIAL MAPPINGS BETWEEN LABELS AND OBJECT FEATURES: SIMULATIONS AND EXPERIMENTS WITH INFANTS

One of the claims of our theoretical framework is that infants preferentially attend to, and consequently encode, relations between dynamic features and that they will do so across a wide range of domains. From our perspective, object labels should be considered as a dynamic feature of an object—they are intermittently available, change state over time, and cannot be encoded from one frame—and this is partly why word learning does not begin in earnest until around 18 months or so (see also Houston & Jusczyk, 2000; Sloutsky & Napolitano, 2003; Strange, 1989). In other words, we suggest that early word learning relies on the information-processing ability to associate two relatively arbitrary dynamic cues, and this capacity is not present until the middle of the second year of life. This is not to say that younger infants are insensitive to labels or that they cannot act as cues to object individuation or categories (Waxman, 2003; Xu, 1999); however, our focus here is on specific aspects of object that infants in the second year of life associate with labels. Our framework makes specific predictions concerning the word–feature relations that infants will learn as they begin to acquire a lexicon.

It is now well established that toward the end of the second year infants assume that labels apply to whole objects rather than to the parts, texture, or color of objects (e.g., Jones & Smith, 1993; Smith et al., 1996, 2002); however, these data were generated from experiments with static objects (c.f. Pulverman, Hirsh-Pasek, Pruden, & Golinkoff, 2006). Our framework makes the prediction that in the presence of moving objects that possess dynamic parts, infants at 18 months of age will associate labels with those parts rather than bodies or motion paths. Thus, infants would initially associate the label "dog" with the legs of a moving dog or the label "car" with the wheels of a moving car. Simulation 3a tested this prediction. A second prediction relates to label learning when global motion is present but not a predictor of category membership. As we discussed earlier, and as was shown in Simulations 1a and 1b, global motion acts as a facilitatory cue to encoding feature correlations. The model predicts, therefore, that in the absence of global motion as a predictor of category membership, the networks will associate labels with a static feature, namely, the body of the objects. Simulation 3b tested this prediction.

SIMULATION 3a

Simulation 3a tested the model's ability to make a prediction regarding the initial mapping between a label and the dynamic features of an object in 18-month-old infants. The networks were habituated to four stimuli in which an extra feature—corresponding to an auditory label—was correlated with the motion and parts but not the body (see Table 8). As in Simulation 2a, the four stimuli could be grouped into two categories on the basis of the relation between the parts and the motion path; however, they could also be categorized on the basis of the relation between the label and the parts and the label and the global motion. During the test phase, the networks were presented with four stimuli: one stimulus included the parts from one category with the motion and label of the other category (*parts switch*), one stimulus included the motion from one category with the parts and label of the other category (*motion switch*), one stimulus included the label from one category with the parts and motion of the other category

TABLE 8

TRAINING AND TESTING SET OF SIMULATION 3A (3B)

	Parts	Motion (body)	Label	Body (motion)
Training trials				
	1	1	1	1
	1	1	1	2
	2	2	2	1
	2	2	2	2
Test trials				
Parts switch	2	1	1	1
Motion (body) switch	1	2	1	2
Label switch	2	2	1	1
Familiar	1	1	1	2

Note.—Each stimulus event possessed four attributes (parts, label, body, and motion path) that could take one of two values. The values for each attribute are represented here as 1s and 2s and were yellow vertically moving parts versus green horizontally moving parts, the word "liff" versus "neem," curvilinear versus rectilinear motion paths, and red curvilinear body versus blue rectilinear body. The test stimuli were composed of familiar attributes that maintained some one relation presented during habituation but violated two other relations. Note that the feature values of the actual habituation and test stimuli were counterbalanced across infants.

(*label switch*), and one stimulus was the same as that presented during habituation (*familiar*). Simulation 3b was identical to Simulation 3a except that the four stimuli could be categorized into two groups on the basis of the correlation between parts, body, and label—global motion was not predictive of category membership.

Procedure

Network Architecture

The simulation used all the training and architecture parameters used to model data for the 18-month-old age group. To implement labels, an extra five-unit input and output group was added to the network with each unit corresponding to a distinct label. This group was connected to the hidden layers in a manner identical to the body, parts, and global motion groups.

Materials

The labels were implemented using orthogonal vectors—during habituation, the unit corresponding to the active label was set to 1, and the rest of the units were set to 0. Two labels were used during habituation, and the remaining three label-units were reserved for pretraining experience.

The training set consisted of four stimuli: the label was correlated with the global motion and moving parts but not the body. We were sensitive to the fact that unlike visual patterns, auditory information is present only briefly in the environment. In view of this, the label input was presented on every third time step. The label target, on the other hand, was active throughout training to encourage the network to form a more robust representation of the label. This implementation was consistent with the notion that once an object is labeled, the label is active in working memory (inasmuch as working memory allows) even when the auditory stimulus itself is no longer present.

Training and Testing

It was important not to make a priori assumptions regarding which aspects of the environment the labels should be correlated with during the pretraining stage. The pretraining corpus therefore contained items in which the labels were correlated with all aspects of the stimulus—body, parts, and global motion. The labels used in the pretraining trials did not correspond to those used in habituation; however, to create overlap between labels (i.e., a sense that labels have something in common—namely, being a label) the non-active labels during the presentation of a given stimulus were partially activated at a level of 0.25. This manipulation turned out not to be critical to the results we report. The habituation training stage and the methods of testing the network were identical to the previously described simulations except for the addition of the labels. Consistent with Sloutsky and Napolitano's (2003) finding that auditory labels, like other dynamic cues, are more salient than static visual stimuli for infants and children, the output errors of the label group were scaled by 10. The testing procedure was identical to the previous simulations.

Results

The behavior of the networks is shown in Figure 12. The networks showed an overall effect of test trial, $F(3, 27) = 185.33$, $p < .0005$. Planned comparisons revealed that compared with the familiar stimuli, there was a reliable increase in error to the label switch test trial, $t(9) = 17.08$, $p < .0005$, and the parts switch test trial, $t(9) = 17.39$, $p < .0005$. There was, however, no increase in error for the motion switch test trial, $t(9) = 1.16$, $p > .3$. Thus, the network showed a reliable increase in error during the two test trials in which the relation between label and parts was violated and showed no increase in error in the test trial when this relation was not changed—evidence that the network was most sensitive to the correlation between the label and parts (Figure 11).

SIMULATION 3b

Procedure

This simulation was identical to Simulation 3a except during the habituation phase, parts, bodies, and label were correlated and global motion was a feature that varied within each category.

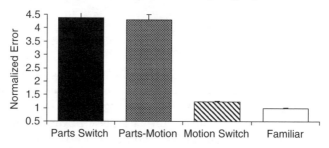

FIGURE 12.—Simulation 3a: Correlating labels with moving parts and global motion.

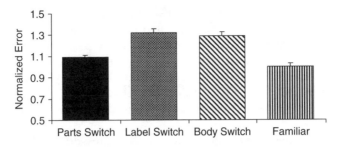

FIGURE 13.—Simulation 3b: Correlating labels with moving parts and object body.

Results

The networks corresponding to the 18-month-old infants showed an overall effect of test type, $F(3, 27) = 18.84$, $p < .0005$ (see Figure 13). Planned comparisons revealed that as in Simulation 3a, the networks showed a reliable increase in error to the label switch trial, $t(9) = 6.42$, $p < .0005$, which violated the label–body and label–parts correlations. The simulation also showed a significant increase in error to the body switch trial, which violated the body–label and body–parts correlations, $t(9) = 5.70$, $p < .0005$. The network did not show a reliable increase in error when presented with the parts switch trial, $t(9) = 1.86$, $p > .2$, which violated the parts–body and parts–label correlations but did not violate the body–label correlation. This dishabituation pattern suggests that when labels are correlated with bodies and parts but not the global motions of the objects, the network is most sensitive to the label–body correlation.

Discussion

The main goal of these simulations was to test a prediction of our theoretical framework regarding the dynamic nature of labels and how they might be associated with features of moving objects. A secondary goal was to demonstrate the domain generality of the underlying principles we proposed. The results of Simulation 3a revealed that, following training on a corpus in which the labels were correlated with moving parts and global motions (both dynamic features), 18-month-old networks associated a novel label with the moving parts of the objects. That the networks did not learn the relation between parts and global motion as they had in the earlier simulations suggests that labels are more salient than global motion. This finding is consistent with the idea that labels have a "privileged" status in early learning but this status arises because labels are dynamic and are presented in the auditory rather than visual input (e.g., Sloutsky & Napolitano, 2003); that is, an object's visual features compete with each other for the network's (and infant's) attention, but object labels face considerably less such competition. When networks were habituated on a corpus in which labels were instead correlated with parts and bodies rather than global motions (Simulation 3b), the networks learned the correlation between the labels and the bodies in the events. This suggests that without the facilitatory effect of the part–motion correlation (see Simulations 1a and 1b), the networks fall back on associating the labels with a static feature—the body.

A second goal of Simulations 3a and 3b was to test our model by making novel predictions about infants' behavior. The current simulation predicted that infants at 18 months of age should preferentially encode the relation between labels and moving object parts when presented with events in which labels are correlated with moving parts and global motion and the bodies are uncorrelated (Simulation 3a). It also predicted that infants at 18 months should be most sensitive to the correlation between labels and bodies when habituated on categories in which the global motion of the stimuli is not correlated with the other features (Simulation 3b). Experiments 1a and 1b were designed to test these predictions.

EXPERIMENTS 1A AND 1B

Experiment 1a was designed to examine which relations among moving parts, global motion, and labels 18-month-old infants encode when these features are presented in a category context. Infants were habituated to four events that corresponded to those presented to the networks in Experiment 3a. The stimuli were visually identical to those used by Rakison (2004, Experiment 1)—that is, the parts and global motion of the objects were invariant but the body was not—but two events were presented in conjunction with one label (i.e., "neem") and two were presented with another label (i.e., "liff"). The objects in the events could therefore be grouped into two categories on the basis of the relation between parts and motion, motion and labels, parts and labels, or all three features. In the test phase, infants were presented with one event in which the parts were switched across the categories (parts switch), one in which the motion was switched across the categories (motion switch), one in which the label was switched across the categories (label switch), and one that was the same as that presented during habituation. Experiment 1b was identical to Experiment 1a with the exception that global motion was not predictive of category membership and instead the four stimuli could be categorized into two groups on the basis of the correlation between parts, body, and label.

Method

Participants

Twelve full-term infants at 18 months of age (mean age 18 months 4 days; range = 17 months 14 days to 18 months 14 days) were participants in this experiment. The majority of infants were White and of middle socioeconomic status. Data from eight additional infants were not included in the final sample, two because of failure to habituate, three because of fussing, two because of experimenter error, and one because of parent interference. This dropout rate ($N = 5$ due to infant behavior) is comparable to that in other habituation studies with 18-month-olds (e.g., Rakison, 2006). Infants were recruited through birth lists obtained from a private company and were given a small gift for their participation.

Stimuli and Design

The habituation and test stimuli were computer-animated events identical to those used by Rakison (2004, Experiment 1) except that a label was presented during each one. During an event, an object with a pair of moving parts and a distinct body with a simple internal shape (e.g., a star) moved from left to right across a screen. The parts were yellow cigar shapes that moved horizontally or green diamond shapes that moved vertically, and the bodies were a red oval shape or a blue pot shape. Each object moved along one of two distinct motion paths—either curvilinear or rectilinear—as it traveled across the screen. An auditory label—either "neem" or "liff"—recorded with a female voice was played every 3 seconds during the event. The events lasted 8 seconds and could be repeated up to three times per trial and between each event a blue screen descended and ascended over a period of approximately 2 seconds. A final stimulus that consisted of a simple causal event with a sheep and a table was used to address issues of infant fatigue.

There were two sets of four events that were used as the habituation stimuli. This made it possible to counterbalance the part–motion–label combinations with body as a variable factor. Six infants in each age group were randomly assigned to one of the two sets. Table 9 shows the full design of the stimulus sets, and it can be seen that values for three of the attributes in the events—namely, parts, motion path, and label—were perfectly correlated in each of the habituation sets. Infants were habituated to four stimuli, two of which exhibited one part–motion–label relation and two of which exhibited another part–motion–label relation.

65

TABLE 9

HABITUATION AND TEST STIMULI USED IN EXPERIMENT 1A (1B) REPRESENTED IN
ABSTRACT NOTATION

	Set A				Set B			
	Parts	Motion (body)	Label	Body (motion)	Parts	Motion (body)	Label	Body (motion)
Habituation stimuli								
	1	1	1	1	1	2	1	1
	1	1	1	2	1	2	1	2
	2	2	2	1	2	1	2	1
	2	2	2	2	2	1	2	2
Test stimuli								
Parts switch	2	1	1	1	2	2	1	1
Motion (body) switch	1	2	1	2	1	1	1	2
Label switch	2	2	1	1	2	1	1	1
Familiar	1	1	1	2	1	2	1	2

Note.—Each stimulus event possessed four attributes (parts, label, body, and motion path) that could take one of two values. The values for each attribute are represented here as 1s and 2s and were yellow vertically moving parts versus green horizontally moving parts, the word "liff" versus "neem," curvilinear versus rectilinear motion paths, and red curvilinear body versus blue rectilinear body. The test stimuli were composed of familiar attributes that maintained some one relation presented during habituation but violated two other relations. Note that the feature values of the actual habituation and test stimuli were counterbalanced across infants.

After habituation, infants were presented with four test events. In one test event, the parts switch, the parts from one object category were paired with the motion and label of the other object category presented during habituation. In a second test event, the motion switch, the motion from one object category was presented with the parts and label of the other object category. In a third test event, the label switch, the label of one object category was presented with the parts and motion of the other object category presented during habituation. The fourth test event, the familiar test, was identical to one of those presented during habituation. The order of the trials was counterbalanced across infants with a Latin Square.

Apparatus and Procedure

Each infant was tested in a quiet, dimly lit laboratory room (approximately 5 m × 4 m) with the events presented on a 43-cm computer monitor. A black curtain surrounded the infant and monitor, and the

66

experimenter coded the infant's visual response on a monitor that received a signal from a closed-circuit video camera situated behind the computer screen. Each infant's looking behavior was recorded for later reliability coding. An Apple G4 computer was used to control the experiment.

The duration of the infant's gaze was recorded by pressing a key on a computer keyboard. At the beginning of the experiment and after each habituation and test trial, a green expanding and contracting circle on a dark background was presented, in conjunction with a bell sound, to capture the infant's attention. Once the infant's gaze was focused on the computer screen, the experimenter began the next trial by pressing a preset key on the computer keyboard. The computer recorded the length of each key press and automatically established when the habituation phase was over and the test phase began.

Infants were tested with a version of the subject-controlled criterion habituation procedure. Each infant sat on their parent's lap facing the computer monitor. During the habituation phase, infants were presented with four distinct events that had various part–motion–label combinations as described in the "Stimuli and Design" section. A trial ended when the infant looked away from the event for over 1 second or until 30 seconds of uninterrupted looking had passed. The habituation phase stopped and the test phase began when an infant's looking time lowered to a set criterion level (a block of three successive trials that were 50% of the total looking time on the first three trials) or until 16 trials had been presented. Before the habituation events, and after the four test events, infants were shown the pretest and posttest stimulus.

Coding and Analyses

The length of each infant's visual fixations were coded by the experimenter's key press and recorded by the computer. A second judge independently recoded 25% of the infants' looking times that were recorded on a videotape. Reliability for infants' looking times was $r > 0.94$, and the mean difference between the two judges coding of infants' looking time on each trial was < 0.3 seconds.

Results

Infants' looking times for the four test trials were analyzed with a repeated-measures ANOVA (parts switch vs. label switch vs. motion switch vs. familiar). The looking times are presented in Figure 14a. There was

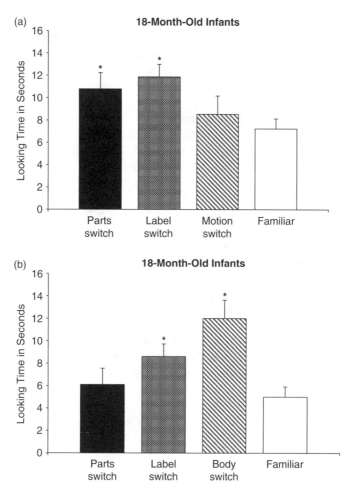

FIGURE 14.—(a) Experiment 1a: infants' looking times (in seconds): a test of Simulation 3a. (b) Experiment 1b: infants' looking times (in seconds): a test of Simulation 3b.

no overall effect of test–trial, $F(3,33) = 1.50$, $p > .2$. However, planned comparisons (one tailed) revealed that infants looked significantly longer at the parts switch test trial ($M = 10.78$, $SD = 8.92$), $F(1,11) = 10.10$, $p < .01$, and the label switch test trial ($M = 11.88$, $SD = 7.11$), $F(1,11) = 3.78$, $p < .05$, than at the familiar test trial ($M = 7.23$, $SD = 4.93$). The analyses also showed that infants looked equally at the motion switch test trial ($M = 8.54$, $SD = 6.68$) than at the familiar test trial, $F(1,11) = 0.29$, $p > .6$ (Figure 13a and b).

EXPERIMENT 1B

Method

Participants

Twelve full-term 18-month-old infants were participants in the experiment, of which seven were boys and five were girls. Data provided by four additional infants were not included in the final sample, three because they failed to habituate and one because of fussing. Infants were recruited in the same way as in the previous experiment.

Stimuli, Apparatus, Design, and Procedure

The stimuli, apparatus, design, and procedure were identical to that used in Experiment 1a; however, in contrast to Experiment 1a infants were habituated to events in which the parts, body, and label of the stimuli were correlated and global motion varied for each of the members of the two categories. The design of the experiment is presented in Table 9.

Results

Infants' visual fixations are illustrated in Figure 14b. A repeated-measures ANOVA (parts switch vs. label switch vs. motion switch vs. familiar) revealed that looking times differed marginally on the four test trials, $F(3, 33) = 2.52$, $p < .08$. Planned comparisons (one tailed) indicated that infants' visual fixations for the label switch test trial ($M = 8.61$, $SD = 7.01$), $F(1, 11) = 3.43$, $p < .05$, and the body switch test trial ($M = 12.02$, $SD = 11.29$), $F(1, 11) = 5.21$, $p < .025$, were significantly higher than for the familiar test trial ($M = 5.05$, $SD = 4.16$). The analyses also showed no significant difference in infants' looking at the parts switch test trial ($M = 6.10$, $SD = 5.34$) than at the familiar test trial, $F(1, 11) = 0.54$, $p > .4$.

Discussion

Experiments 1a and 1b were designed to test the predictions generated by the network concerning how infants associate labels with specific features of moving objects. Consistent with the networks' behavior, infants in Experiment 1a at 18 months of age encoded the relation between parts and labels—that is, they looked longer at the two switch trials that violated these correlations—and did not learn the relation between parts and motion or

69

motion and labels. Also consistent with the networks, infants in Experiment 1b encoded the relation between labels and bodies but not those between labels and parts or parts and bodies.

The pattern of findings supports the view that labels are a dynamic and salient feature of objects that may have a "privileged" status in early learning. We suggest that this privileged status arises not because of some predisposition to learn language on the part of the infant but rather from the fact that labels are dynamic, are a unique and perfect predictor of category membership, and face little competition for attention compared with the many features of objects that are presented in the visual input. The data also suggest that when global motion is a predictive feature of category membership, this facilitates infants' attention to the relation between labels and other dynamic features (e.g., moving parts). In the absence of such a facilitating cue, however, infants associate labels with static features (e.g., the bodies of objects). One implication of this finding is that in the presence of moving objects infants and toddlers may not generalize labels on the basis of shape (e.g., Smith et al., 1996, 2002) but instead may use dynamic features as the basis for such generalization.

Our model does not make any unique predictions about the auditory nature of labels. The model would make the same predictions of labels presented in other modalities. Neither does it require labels to be words. This is consistent with our theoretical stance. We hold that basic-level labels have two unique properties: they are highly predictive of category membership, and they systematically refer to categories. In other words, once infants learn that "dog" refers to the category of dogs and "cats" refers to the category of cats, they develop the assumption that a novel word also refers to a category of things. This view is closely aligned to that of Colunga and Smith (2002) who argued that a name is a bundle of features co-occurring with categories. In this view, infants learn to associate particular kinds of stimuli with labels because only some stimuli are predictably and systematically correlated with categories. It is also supported by a number of studies on early word learning. Woodward and Hoyne (1999), for example, found that 13-month-old infants treat both words and non-verbal sounds as possible names, whereas 20-month-olds treated only words as names. Namy and Waxman (1998) similarly found that 18-month-old infants associated both novel words and novel gestures with categories but that 26-month-olds associated only novel words with categories. Colunga and Smith (2002) hypothesized that in addition to spoken words, animal and vehicle sounds are also predictably and systematically correlated with categories, and so children should associate such sounds with the appropriate category. This hypothesis was confirmed in 20- and 26-month-old children.

70

SUMMARY OF SIMULATIONS 1–3 AND EXPERIMENTS 1A–B

The simulations presented thus far demonstrate the ability of a domain-general associative learning mechanism to account for a range of data in the context of encoding correlations between static and dynamic features. Simulations 1a and 1b showed that motion, while difficult to process, can act as a facilitatory cue in that it helps the model to encode the correlation between the moving parts and global motion of the stimulus. Simulation 1c showed that when younger infants' behavior is modeled, they are at first unable to encode dynamic features in motion events but are sensitive to static features such as the body of a stimulus. Simulation 2a showed that, like infants (Rakison, 2004), the model has more difficulty with encoding dynamic correlations in a category context, and it is not until 22 months of age or until it is able to encode the relation between dynamic parts and a global motion trajectory. Simulation 2b showed that, consistent with previous work with infants, the model representing the 22-month-olds failed to encode the relation between the body of an object and its motion trajectory. Simulations 3a and 3b showed that the networks predict that infants will associate labels with dynamic parts and with object bodies depending on whether global motion is predictive of category membership. Experiments 1a and 1b revealed that these predictions were supported by 18-month-olds' behavior in a task comparable to that given to the networks in Simulations 3a and 3b.

The experiments presented thus far have demonstrated that an instantiation of a number of features of our theory can lead to the development of object concepts in networks that match those, at least in terms of behavior, formed by infants. Simulations 4 and 5 tested more directly the ability of the current model to generate constraints on learning based on previously experienced relations between features and motion characteristics. To address this issue, the model was exposed to training stimuli in the contexts of objects' role in a causal event (Simulation 4) and objects' ability to move without an external physical cause (Simulation 5). They were then tested with novel stimuli that either maintained or violated the regularities they learned from the training stimuli. The simulations were designed to match as closely as possible experimental work by Rakison (2005a, 2006).

VI. SIMULATION 4: A MODEL OF RAKISON, 2005A: ANIMACY RELATIONS IN CAUSAL EVENTS

Rakison (2005a) habituated 12-, 14-, and 16-month-old infants with Michotte-like causal events in which one geometric figure moved toward and contacted another geometric figure, "causing" the second figure to start moving. It was reasoned that in the real world agents tend to be animates and have moving parts, and it is more common that they cause motion in inanimate objects that tend not to have moving parts. With this in mind, Rakison (2005a) habituated infants on either events consistent with these real-world regularities—those in which the agent had a moving part and the recipient had a static part—or those that are inconsistent with these regularities in which the opposite relation held; that is, the agent possessed a static part and the recipient possessed a moving part. In the test phase, infants were presented with a familiar event that was identical to that seen during habituation as well as a switch event in which the agent possessed a static part and the recipient possessed the dynamic part. Illustrations of the events are presented in Figure 15.

Rakison (2005a) predicted that younger infants, who have not yet learned the regularities common in the real world, would be unconstrained in the relations between parts and causal role (i.e., agent or recipient) that they would encode, whereas older infants would encode only those relations that are consistent with their previous experience; that is, when agents possessed dynamic parts and recipients possessed static parts. The results of the experiments confirmed this prediction: 12-month-olds failed to encode any of the relations in the events, 14-month-olds encoded all of the relations to which they were exposed, and 16-month-olds encoded only those relations that conformed to those in the real world. Here, we attempted to extend the network we developed to account for learning to correlate dynamic and static features (Simulations 1–3), to the learning of simple causal events. Our main goal was to see whether applying the CAAL framework to Michotte-like causal learning would produce the kind of developmental trajectory observed by Rakison (2005a)—an initial insensitivity to whether

72

A Habituation/Familiar   **B Switch**

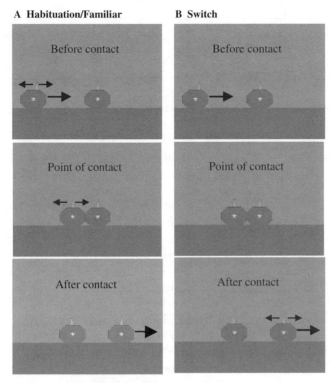

FIGURE 15.—Example of stimulus events in Rakison (2005a). Similar events were presented to the CAAL framework in Simulations 4 and 5.
Note.—Reprinted from the *Journal of Experimental Child Psychology, 91*, David H. Rakison, A secret agent? How infants learn about the identity of objects in a causal scene, pp. 271–296, Copyright (2005), with permission from Elsevier.

agents or recipients are more likely to possess moving parts, to an "acceptance" of pairings both consistent and inconsistent with real-world regularities, to, finally, learning the consistent relationship, but showing resistance to learning the inconsistent (static-agent/moving-patient) relationship.

METHOD

Network Architecture

The model that instantiated the CAAL framework was extended to the paradigm used by Rakison (2005a). The most notable change was to the input/output groups, which were modified to allow us to present information about two objects simultaneously (dubbed "agent" and "patient" in the

73

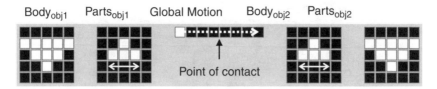

Body_{obj1}   Parts_{obj1}   Global Motion   Body_{obj2}   Parts_{obj2}

Point of contact

FIGURE 16.—Inputs for Simulations 4 and 5. The parts move with a cycle of three time-steps; global motion cycles every seven time-steps.

empirical studies). The input and output layers for the network used in this simulation consisted of a global motion group representing the location of the object currently in motion, and two groups representing the body and part layers for each of the two objects—a total of five input and five output groups. Figure 16 shows these input layers. Notice that each of the two objects has its own body and parts layer, but there is a single global motion layer that represents the motion of the currently active object. As in the earlier simulations, nothing about these input groups explicitly marks them as "body" or "part"—just as nothing in the real world explicitly labels object parts as parts. Bodies and parts are defined schematically through their roles in the scene. The parts for the objects were identical

Before the midpoint, marked "point of contact," the currently active object is the one on the left in Figure 16. Following contact, the right object starts moving. There is no explicit representation of "active object" in the network. Rather, what is meant by "active" is that for an object with moving parts, the parts would start moving (and have increased perceptual salience) only before the contact point for the first object, and only after the contact point for the second object. Both objects were visible to the network throughout the duration of the trial. This reflects the procedure used by Rakison (2005a).

Materials

The stimuli were based on those in Rakison's (2005a) study with 12- to 16-month-old infants. The global motion was smooth and continuous and the two objects had identical parts and bodies. For the pretraining phase, we generated six new stimuli with novel bodies and parts. Four of these stimuli involved an agent with a dynamic part and a recipient with a static part and two had the reverse part-causal role relation. The former were presented to the network with much greater probability than the latter (95% vs. 5%), in accordance with the assumption that infants experience objects with dynamic parts acting as agents and objects with static parts acting as recipients far more commonly than the converse (a series of additional simulations that used different ratios are presented below).

74

TABLE 10

PARAMETERS USED IN SIMULATION 4

Age (months)	Hidden Units (FL/SL)	Pretraining Epochs	Habituation Epochs	Weight Decay
12	5/20	0	20	0.04
14	8/20	50	20	0.01
16	9/20	150	20	0.0025

Training

Part motion was represented as actual motion of the activity pattern in the appropriate input and output group. In accord with the assumption that motion captures the attention of infants, the output derivative of the group was scaled by a constant of 10 whenever the part was moving. The errors of the global motion group were scaled by a factor of 15. Both of these values were the same as those used in the previous simulations reported here. Habituation consisted of a single stimulus event depicting two identical objects. In the consistent condition, the first object (the agent) had a moving part and the second object (the recipient) had a static part. In the inconsistent condition, the relation was reversed: The agent now had a static part and the recipient had a moving one.

Because the size of the input layers and complexity of the task was different from that of the previous experiments, the number of habituation trials was different in the current simulation (Table 10). All of the other architectural and training parameters were exactly the same as in the previous experiments.

RESULTS

The results of the simulations are illustrated in Figure 17. The simplest networks, used to model the performance of 12-month-old infants, showed no sensitivity to the difference between agents with static or moving parts, $F(1,9) < 1$, NS. That is, after being habituated to either the agent with a dynamic part and the recipient with the static part or the agent with the static part and the recipient with the dynamic part, these networks did not show a reliable increase in error when presented with stimuli that involved the opposite part-causal role relations.

The 14-month-old networks, in contrast, learned relations that were both consistent and inconsistent with the regularities found in the real world (in this case, the training set). Thus, the networks that were habituated to agents with a dynamic part and a recipient with a static part showed increased error to the converse event, $F(1,9) = 480.12$, $p < .0005$, and the

75

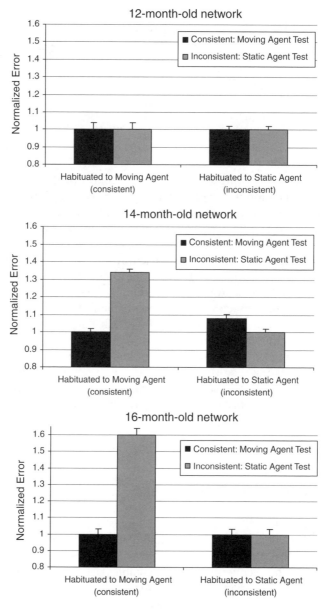

FIGURE 17.—Simulation 4: (Rakison, 2005a): Animacy relations in causal events.

networks that were habituated to agents with a static part and a recipient with a dynamic part revealed a significant increase in error when tested with the opposite part-causal role relations, $F(1, 9) = 152.02$, $p < .0005$.

The more sophisticated 16-month-old networks, which had greater prior experience of agents with dynamic parts and recipients with static parts, did not dishabituate to the agent with a dynamic part and recipient with a static part after they were habituated to the agent with a static part and the recipient with a moving part—the relation inconsistent with the real world—$F(1, 9) < 1$. However, the networks showed a significant increase in error to an agent with a static part and a recipient with a moving part after being habituated to the opposite relations $F(1, 9) = 2033.39, p < .0005$. The interaction with training type (consistent vs. inconsistent) as a between-network factor and testing type (consistent vs. inconsistent) as a within-network factor was highly significant, $F(1, 18) = 852.13, p < .0005$.

The pattern of results obtained by performing separate F-tests on the networks modeling different ages and habituation conditions was mirrored by cross-simulation analyses with age and training type as between-network factors and test-trial as a within-network factor. For the networks trained on trials consistent with the real world (i.e., agents have moving parts), there was a significant age × test-trial interaction, $F(2, 27) = 742.89, p < .0005$, showing progressively greater sensitivity to the first object (i.e., the agent) possessing a moving part. For the networks trained on trials inconsistent with the real world (i.e., patients, but not agents have moving parts), there was also a significant age × test-trial interaction, $F(2, 27) = 22.05, p < .0005$, now showing that only the intermediate 14-month-old networks were sensitive to the inconsistent pattern.

VARYING THE PRETRAINING EXPERIENCE

One assumption we made in the present simulation was that infant experience includes many more events with animate agents (i.e., agents with moving parts) compared with inanimate agents (i.e., agents with static parts). Specifically, the ratio used in the pretraining experience was 95% of the former and 5% of the latter. A question worth asking is what effect varying this ratio has on subsequent learning.[5] An immediate prediction is if prior experience includes an equal ratio of animate-agent and inanimate-agent events, then the models simulating performance of 18-month-old infants should retain the flexibility required to learn both the animate-agent and inanimate-agent. This is depicted in the 50–50% condition in Figure 18. The network is now sensitive to both as measured by significant increases in error to the inanimate-agent trial when habituated to the animate-agent, $F(1, 9) = 339.70, p < .0005$ (the normally consistent condition), and to the animate-agent trial when habituated to the inanimate-agent (the normally inconsistent condition), $F(1, 9) = 15.30, p < .0005$. The habituation

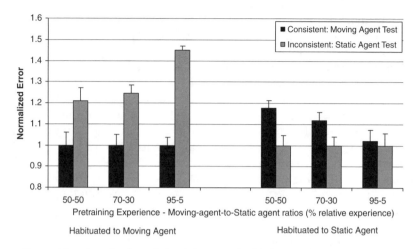

FIGURE 18.—A replication of Simulation 4 with dishabituation modulated by varying pretraining experience [(50–50 corresponds to prior equal exposure to animate agents (i.e., agents with moving parts)] inanimate agents (i.e., agents with static parts); 95–5 corresponds to 95% exposure to animate agents and 5% exposure to inanimate agents.

condition × testing-type interaction is highly significant, $F(1,9) = 359.06$, $p < .0005$. The size of the dishabituation is slightly, but not significantly, larger when networks are habituated to the agent-animate trial, compared with when habituated to the agent-inanimate trial, two-sample t-test, $t(18) = 1.53, p = .14$.

The networks in the 70–30% condition also retain sensitivity to both relations, but now the greater experience with the animate-agent trials creates a more obvious asymmetry: the dishabituation to the inanimate-agent (inconsistent) when trained on the animate-agent (consistent) is .24, which is significantly greater than the dishabituation to the animate-agent test-trial (consistent) when habituated on the inanimate-agent (.12), two-sample t-test, $t(18) = 6.29, p < .0005$. The 95–5% condition replicates the pattern seen earlier (Figure 17, bottom panel). Overall, we find that the increasing asymmetry in prior experience between the agent-animate and agent-inanimate trials produces a significant ratio × habituation condition × testing trial, with ratio and habituation condition as between-network factors, and testing trial as a within-network factor, $F(2,54) = 6.54, p < .01$.

DISCUSSION

Simulation 4 was designed to examine the emergence of constraints on learning through prior experience in the context of simple causal events.

Within this context, the model captured the developmental trend displayed by 12-, 14-, and 16-month-old infants in the studies by Rakison (2005a). Between 12 and 16 months, infants, as well as networks in the current simulations showed a progression from being insensitive to relations involving parts and an object's causal role, to encoding all relations between causal role and the parts of an object, to encoding only relations consistent with their previous experience with those in the real world. This result is particularly notable given that the parameters used were taken directly from the earlier simulations in this monograph in which the model was being trained on entirely different types of relations. This demonstrates that the same basic learning mechanism can account for how infants learn about the different kinds of objects that move along distinct motion trajectories and that play distinct roles in causal events.

Despite the greater computational flexibility of the older networks given their greater number of hidden units and lower weight decay, these networks were actually more constrained in learning relations inconsistent with prior experience. This reduction of plasticity over time has to do with entrenchment of previously learned material (for a discussion see Munakata & McClelland, 2003). Simply stated, as a network learns, its connection weights grow larger and are more resistant to change. Although the habituation stimuli were not identical to the pretraining stimuli, the use of the same connection weights for both meant that greater connection weights resulting from more prior experience have a greater effect in constraining the learning of the stimuli used in habituation. In particular, we showed that the system becomes increasingly biased to learn new stimuli with dynamic agents and static recipients—relations consistent to those learned during pretraining. The importance of prior experience in constraining learning is further demonstrated by an additional set of simulations in which we varied the relative ratio of events involving animate and inanimate agents (as modeled by agents with moving or static parts). The more equal the ratio of the two types of relations, the more sensitivity the network retains as reflected by being able to learn both types of relations.

NOTE

5. We thank an anonymous reviewer for this suggestion.

VII. SIMULATION 5: A MODEL OF RAKISON, 2006: ANIMACY RELATIONS IN NONCAUSAL EVENTS

Rakison (2006) demonstrated that the emergence of constraints on learning of the kind evidenced in Rakison (2005a) is not limited to causal events. Infants at 16, 18, and 20 months of age were habituated to simple noncausal events in which a geometric figure with a dynamic part started to move without physical contact from an identical figure with a static part. Infants were then tested on events that either maintained or switched the part relations in the events. Because inanimate objects generally do not start moving on their own and because animacy is correlated with having moving parts, the relation consistent with real-world experience is the one in which the second object has moving parts. Rakison (2006) found that the youngest infants did not encode the animacy relation at all, the 18-month-old infants encoded relations both consistent and inconsistent with those in the real world, and the oldest infants encoded only the relations consistent with those in the real world. Interestingly, although the data showed the same developmental pattern of sensitivity to animacy in the context of noncausal events as with causal events (Rakison, 2005a, and Simulation 4), the pattern for the noncausal events was delayed compared with causal events. Instead of the trend occurring between 12 and 16 months in the causal context, it occurred between 16 and 20 months in the noncausal context.

The current simulation had two aims. First, the simulation was designed to examine whether the model would show a developmental pattern similar to Simulation 4 when habituated to noncausal events (specifically those not involving direct contact between the two objects). Second, it was used to determine whether the pattern of constrained learning in a noncausal context would be developmentally delayed in comparison with a causal context, as was the case in the empirical studies reported by Rakison (2006).

METHOD

Network Architecture

The network architecture developed in Simulation 5; the developmental parameters were adapted for the age groups used by Rakison (2006). Notice that in the present simulation the 16-month-old infants are represented by the very same architecture (number of hidden units, and weight-decay parameter) as those in Simulation 4.

Materials

The pretraining corpus used the current simulation included items for which the motion of the first object was interrupted by a spatial and temporal gap (Chaput & Cohen, 2001) after which the second object started to move. The first object either had moving or static parts (50% probability of each), while the second object always had moving parts (i.e., the "recipients" of a noncausal action were always self-propelled). Note that the networks have no sense of causality in a conceptual sense—the difference between events with a direct motion and events in which there is a temporal or spatial gap in the motion is purely perceptual in the current simulation (see Lupyan & Rakison, 2006 for an extension of this into the "conceptual" realm).

Training and Testing

The procedure for training and testing the networks was identical to the previous simulations. The networks were habituated to a single habituation stimulus exhibiting noncausal (gap+delay) motion and either a first object with a static part and a second object with a moving part (consistent condition) or a first object with a moving part and a second object with a static part (inconsistent condition). The networks were then tested on both relations, and the errors recorded. The networks, as was the case for infants in the studies by Rakison (2005a, 2006), exhibited slightly faster habituation to the noncausal trials compared with the causal ones. For this reason, the number of habituation trials in the current simulation was reduced to 10 compared with 20 used in Simulation 4 (see Table 11).

RESULTS

The behavior of the networks during the testing phase is illustrated in Figure 19. The networks used to model the performance of 16-month-olds showed no sensitivity to the switch between the part of first object and the

TABLE 11

Age (months)	Hidden Units (FL/SL)	Pretraining Epochs	Habituation Epochs	Weight Decay
16	9/20	75	10	0.0025
18	10/20	150	10	0.001
20	12/20	400	10	0.00075

second object in the context of the noncausal gap+delay global motion. There was no reliable difference in the error between the two test trials when habituated to either the consistent relation stimulus, $F(1, 9) < 1, p > .3$, or the inconsistent relation, $F(1, 9) = 1.09, p > .3$.

The networks modeling the performance of 18-month-olds showed sensitivity to both relations. When habituated to the relation consistent with that in the real world, the networks showed a reliable increase when tested on the opposite, inconsistent relation, $F(1, 9) = 39.76$, $p < .0005$ (though there was large between-network variance as indicated by the errors bars—Figure 19 middle—the within-network difference between the familiar and the switch trial was highly reliable). When habituated to the inconsistent relation, the networks again showed an increase in error when tested on the opposite, consistent relation, $F(1, 9) = 11.89 \, p < .01$. The interaction with training type (consistent vs. inconsistent) as a between-network factor and testing type (consistent vs. inconsistent) as a within-network factor was highly significant, $F(1, 18) = 58.93, p < .0005$.

In contrast to the 18-month-old networks, the networks modeling the performance of 20-month-olds showed an increase in error to the inconsistent relation when habituated to the consistent relation, $F(1, 9) = 88.20, p < .0005$, but they did not show an increase in error when habituated to the inconsistent relation and tested on the consistent relation, $F(1, 9) = 2.04$, $p > .1$. The statistical differences between the 18- and the 20-month-old networks were largely attributable to lower variability in the latter networks. That is, different starting weights seemed to have a larger effect on the performance of the 18-month-old networks and less effect on the 20-month-old networks.

For completeness, we supplement the within-network F-tests above, with cross-simulation analyses with age and training type as between-network factors and test-trial as a within-network factor. For the networks trained on trials consistent with the real world (i.e., a self-propelled object with moving parts), there was a significant age × test-trial interaction, $F(2, 27) = 15.53$, $p < .0005$, showing greater sensitivity for the two 18- and 20-month-old networks compared with the 16-month-old networks. For

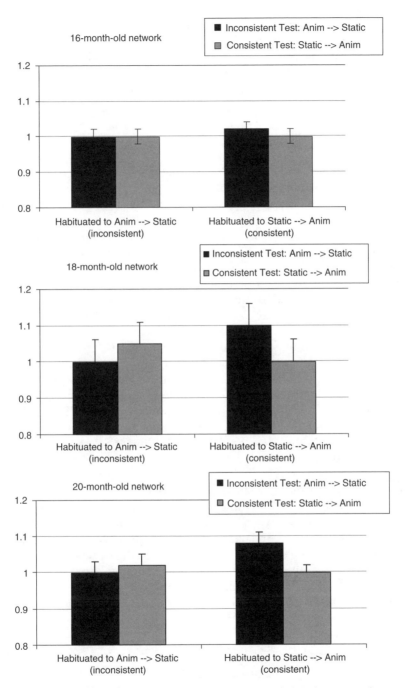

FIGURE 19.—Simulation 5: (Rakison, 2006): Animacy relations in noncausal events.

the networks trained on trials inconsistent with the real world (i.e., a self-propelled object without moving parts), there was also a significant age × test-trial interaction, $F(2, 27) = 3.94$, $p < .05$, showing that only the intermediate 18-month-old networks were sensitive to the inconsistent pattern.

DISCUSSION

Recall that Rakison (2005a) showed that it was not until 16 months of age that infants exhibited sensitivity to the appropriate feature-causal role relations that are found in the real world, and that Rakison (2006) found that it was not until 20 months of age that infants show the same sensitivity to feature relations involved in self-propulsion. Thus, 16-month-olds, and therefore presumably 18-month-olds, were constrained by prior experience when tested in a causal context, but learned both consistent and inconsistent relations in the noncausal context involving self-propulsion. The networks in Simulations 4 and 5 replicated this developmental pattern.

The networks offer an account of why the developmental pattern revealed for 12- to 16-month-old infants in a causal context was shifted to 16- to 20-month-olds in the noncausal context. Consider that before the point of contact, the networks (and presumably the infants) cannot differentiate between causal and noncausal motion because the two are identical. It is only when there is either contact or a lack of contact between the two objects that the determination of "causality" or of "self-propulsion" can be made. In the case of a causal action, it is the first object that "informs" the network of whether the stimulus and its features are consistent or not with those in the real world. If it has moving parts, it is consistent with prior experience. If the parts are static, it is inconsistent. On the other hand, for a noncausal action the first object can have either moving or static parts. It is the second object that is informative, having either moving parts in the consistent condition, or static parts in the inconsistent condition (the assumption is that the second object must be self-propelled to move without an external cause). The reason, therefore, that the developmental pattern is delayed in the noncausal context is that it takes both more prior experience and a more sophisticated architecture to learn which object is more informative.

VIII. GENERAL DISCUSSION

One of the most impressive cognitive accomplishments in early development is children's ability to representationally carve nature at its joints. By preschool age, children understand that one broad group of things in the world—what adults label as "animates"—possess specific surface features (e.g., legs, eyes), internal biological properties (e.g., hearts, brains), and psychological states (e.g., goals, desires). At the same time, preschoolers also know that another broad group of things in the world—what adults label as "inanimates"—possess different surface features and internal properties and do not possess mental states. It is generally agreed that a crucial first step in developing such concepts involves learning about objects' and entities' static and dynamic features, or in other words, how things appear and how they move (e.g., Mandler, 2003; Quinn & Eimas, 1997). Our aim in this monograph was to show that general processes such as associative learning can account for how infants acquire concepts that incorporate both static and dynamic features of objects. We presented a theoretical framework that outlined how such processes, in combination with simple inherent attention biases and information-processing and neurological maturation, can lead to concepts that augment over time with ever more complex information about the static and dynamic features of objects and entities. We also proposed that the process of encoding relations of the statistical regularities that exist in the real world leads to the emergence of constraints on future learning.

The simulations reported here show that general learning processes, in combination with a few well-supported assumptions about development and attention in the first years of life and the structure of the input, are sufficient to account for how and when infants learn about the surface features of objects as well as about how they move in the world. The networks across the simulations displayed the same developmental progressions observed in 10- to 22-month-old infants in a number of experimental tasks (Rakison, 2004, 2005a, 2006; Rakison & Poulin-Dubois, 2002), and they made specific predictions about word learning in

18-month-olds that were borne out by original empirical data. In so doing, the network exhibited behavior that appears, on the surface, to show that it had formed an "abstract" representation of objects that encapsulates their movement characteristics; however, the networks' "looking time" behavior was based solely on the strength of connection weights between correlations of static and dynamic features. The model was capable of learning about the static features of objects as well as how those objects move and it was not necessary to implement prior knowledge, specialized processes, or specialized architectures to accomplish these tasks (see, e.g., Baillargeon, 2001; Gelman, 1990; Mandler, 1992, 2003; Premack, 1990; Spelke, 1994). In the following sections, we discuss implications of these findings for the nature and development of concepts that include objects' movement capabilities as well their psychological and internal, nonobvious properties. We also outline potential criticisms of our model as well as highlight some prospective future directions for infant research and modeling.

MECHANISMS OF EARLY CONCEPT DEVELOPMENT

According to one prominent view, the complexity of the input, among other things, implies that concept formation must be supported by specialized, domain-specific mechanisms (Baillargeon, 1999; Gelman, 1990; Gelman et al., 1995; Leslie, 1995; Mandler, 1992, 2003; Pauen, 2002; Spelke, 1994). The theorists who adopt this perspective vary in their claims of the exact mechanisms involved; yet they have in common the idea that early categorization and induction is based on top-down knowledge of properties not readily available in the perceptual input (e.g., how things move, category membership) and that infants' relatively rapid representational progress means that such knowledge can only develop with the aid of specialized mechanisms, modules, or skeletal principles.

We proposed an alternative view of early object concept development. At the heart of this view is that idea that general processes such as associate learning are sufficiently powerful to extract both the static and dynamic featural regularities that demarcate animals, people, and insects from furniture, tools, vehicles, and plants. We consider associative processes to be an excellent contender for this task for some of the same reasons highlighted by Colunga and Smith (2005a) in their discussion of word learning. First, associative learning is ubiquitous among animals, and its presence in infants and children is beyond dispute and well understood; second, it is a powerful mechanism for extracting statistical regularities from a noisy input such as that exhibited by the features of animates and inanimates in the world.

The simulations reported here support the view that associative processes can lead to representations that encapsulate both the surface features of objects as well as how they move along different motion paths, the role they play in causal events, and whether or not they are self-propelled. Indeed, that the same simple recurrent network architecture can account for learning across a number of relatively distinct movement characteristics, as well as word learning, provides further support for the notion that one mechanism—namely, an associative one—may underlie infants' ability to encode them. In this respect, the simulations reported here are among the first to provide a demonstration of what Munakata (2006) has called "all-purpose models"; that is, our model is capable of processing appropriately a variety of kinds of information across a range of tasks.

One argument against associative learning as the primary mechanism for concept development for objects and entities is that it is too unconstrained. This *insufficiency of constraints* or *Original Sim* argument is that animates and inanimates involve so many correlations that a priori it is not possible to identify which ones are significant for category membership and which are not. We agree that associative learning alone is insufficiently constrained to allow infants to form veridical representations for the objects and entities around them (Rakison, 2003). As a solution to this issue, and based on the extant literature, we suggested that newborns' attention biases direct them to attend to dynamic over static cues, relatively large stimuli or features over relatively small stimuli or features (Slater et al., 1990), and relatively complex over relatively simple stimuli (Kaplan & Werner, 1986; Slater, 1989).

These attention biases mean that not all correlations in the world are perceived equally; that is, infants are more likely to encode correlations involving, for example, larger features because they are more likely to fixate on them than correlations that involve smaller features. We implemented only one of these attention biases in the simulations—the preference to attend dynamic over static cues—because our goal was show that associative processes can account for concepts that incorporate motion properties of objects. This bias facilitates the learning of dynamic features, but sometimes at the expense of learning about static features (Figure 6). As Simulations 1a and 1b showed, including moving parts in a stimulus facilitated the learning of the correlations between dynamic features. The reason for this is that the inclusion of moving parts increases the "coherent covariation" of the stimulus (Rogers & McClelland, 2004) and results in representations that reflect feature correlations instead of just the individual features.

A second argument levied against associative processes as the mechanism for concept development is that the association of static and dynamic features cannot lead to a concept or "meaning" of what something is.

For instance, Mandler (2003) claimed that "it seems difficult to understand how merely associating percepts with each other can result in concept formation" (p. 105). According to this approach, the role of specialized mechanisms—be they processes such as perceptual analysis or domain-specific modules—is to interpret observed perceptual information and re-code it into a more abstract, conceptual version. In this way, the perception of a dog triggers the concept of "animal," which triggers information about how an animal can move, whether it offers support, and so on.

Our associative learning perspective is irreconcilable with this position. Learning, according to our view, does not lead to the development of abstract concepts of "animate" and "inanimate" in the first 18 or 24 months of life, as some theorists argue is the case (e.g., Mandler, 2003). Although infants' categorization and induction behavior may give the appearance that they possess abstract concepts of this nature (e.g., Mandler et al., 1991; Mandler & McDonough, 1998), we argue that there is no need to ascribe such adult-like representations to the young mind. Instead, associative mechanisms give rise to representations of correlations of features and it is the strength of the association between features that defines to what extent they determine category membership. The simulations reported here illustrate how this process would operate. The representations the network formed are sensitive to the features and motion characteristics that are typical of animates and inanimates (e.g., agents possess moving parts) but nowhere in this learning process does the network (and by extension, the child) need to rely on top-down abstract principles of animacy or causality. This is not to say, however, that such knowledge does not emerge at some point in development. As we discuss in the section "The Role of Labeling on Early Concepts," we believe that the emergence of language in the young child plays a crucial role in the onset of more accessible, abstract knowledge.

WHAT ABOUT DEVELOPMENT?

After over 30 years of research of early concept formation, there are now some well-established and accepted developmental trends in infants' categorization and induction. For example, using distinct experimental paradigms it has been shown that infants undergo a global-to-basic shift whereby they categorize at a more general level (e.g., animals vs. vehicles) before they categorize at a more specific level (e.g., cats vs. dogs) (Behl-Chadha, 1996; Mandler et al., 1991; Quinn, 2004; Quinn et al., 1993). It has also been demonstrated that infants cannot initially parse individual features of objects or events, after which they can encode individual features of objects or events but not relations among those features, after which they are able to encode relations among features in a discrimination context, and lastly they can encode such relations when they are embedded in a category context (Rakison, 2004; Rakison & Poulin-Dubois, 2002; Younger & Cohen, 1986). In our view, it is imperative that any theory of early object concept formation explain why infants display these, and other, progressions from a developmental standpoint; that is, what changes occur in the infant across time that allows increasingly complex information to be incorporated into existing representations.

Our first claim about development was a more general one about the nature of concept acquisition. We proposed that development is a continuous process with novel information that the infant encodes being augmented to that which is already represented (see also Quinn & Eimas, 1997). According to this view, putative discontinuities in learning and behavior do not result from the activation or "triggering" of specific mechanisms or modules (e.g., Leslie, 1995), but instead come about due to gradual, quantitative changes in representations. Our second claim about development was more specific. We suggested that the basic mechanisms of learning do not change over developmental time. Instead, we proposed that change in concept acquisition skills in infancy is underpinned by general advances in information-processing abilities (e.g., faster encoding, improving short- and long-term memory), and, more speculatively, neurological maturation of the hippocampus and communication between the dorsal and ventral visual streams. The complexities of development cannot be explained with so few parameters and the claim here is not that these are the only ones that contribute to infants' developing concept acquisition skills. At the same time, however, the available evidence implies that they are strong contenders as powerful factors that lead to advances in infants' ability to encode the information that they encounter.

Because the view that development is a continuous process is implicit to connectionist models, the simulations reported here explicitly incorporated aspects of information-processing advances and neurological maturation to establish whether they could account for the changes in behavior observed in previous empirical work (e.g., Rakison, 2004, 2005a, 2006; Rakison & Poulin-Dubois, 2002). Specifically, we increased over time the number of hidden units and reduced the weight-decay parameter of the fast learning links in the network. The former allowed the network to encode more information and be more sensitive to the details of the training set, and the latter allowed the network to integrate the information from the habituation stimuli with that learned previously. In conjunction, these parameters implemented a very simple model of neural maturation of working memory.

The results of the simulations support the idea that these implementations can account for a number of developmental progressions involving infants' ability to encode static and dynamic cues. For example, in

89

Simulations 1 and 2 the simulations showed the same developmental trend as that observed in Rakison and Poulin-Dubois (2002) and Rakison (2004); that is, 10-month-old networks encoded the body of moving objects but not correlations among features, 14-month-old networks encoded relations among dynamic local and global features for two objects, 18-month-old networks encoded all of the feature relations for two objects, and 22-month-old networks encoded relations between dynamic cues in a category context. Though the quantitative predictions of the model depend on the parameter values used (see, e.g., Table 3), the qualitative pattern is quite robust and is present for a variety of parameter values. Our results are also not dependent on the exact implementation of development—increasing the number of FL units and lowering weight-decay. For example, the pattern observed in Simulations 1a and 1b—14-month-olds only dishabituating in the presence of moving parts, and 18-month-olds dishabituating to more switch trials in the presence of moving parts—can be obtained by exposing the "older" networks to more habituation trials under the assumption that older infants extract more information during the habituation session compared with younger infants. The conclusion in both cases is much the same: the differences in sensitivity to dynamic correlations result from differences in information-processing ability. We hypothesize that this difference results from increases in working memory capacity and the increased use of previous experience to guide learning (e.g., Simulations 4 and 5), but the qualitative pattern of our results does not depend on the particular instantiation of these mechanisms used in the present model.

The simulations in Simulations 4 and 5 showed a developmental trend of increasingly constrained learning identical to that in Rakison (2005a, 2006). As predicted by our framework, younger networks showed no sensitivity to the relations between specific features and an object's causal role or onset of motion; older networks learned all relations—even those inconsistent with the "real world" (as defined by the training set)—between features and causal role or onset of motion; and still older networks learned only those relations between features and motion characteristics that were consistent with the "real world." This general developmental progression was particularly significant because it showed that the network's experience with items that exhibit specific property relations leads to the emergence of representations that constrain future learning and generalization. Because such emergent constraints have been discovered in early concept acquisition across a range of domains (see Madole & Cohen, 1995; Namy et al., 2004; Stager & Werker, 1997), we suggest that they might arise whenever an associative learning mechanism extracts regularities from a noisy input. This is not to say that representations that are formed via other forms of learning cannot also give rise to this effect (see Murphy, 2002). Instead, we suggest that the appearance of this developmental progression, in infancy at least, may be an indicator that associatively acquired representations are influencing or constraining which aspects of novel information is encoded.

The pattern of increasingly constrained learning depended on the network having two parallel learning systems—one quick learning but fragile, the other slow learning and more permanent. This idea of complimentary learning systems is inspired by the hippocampal–cortical model of McClelland et al. (1995), which presented a mechanism that avoids catastrophic interference in a connectionist network in a neurally plausible way. While our implementation of fast-learning and slow-learning units invites comparison with the hippocampal–cortical system, the present model is too simple to evaluate such a comparison. The purpose of implementing FL and SL units in the current model was to allow the network to maintain a "long-term" memory of prior experiences, while being able to learn stimuli presented in the habituation phase. A consequence of this implementation is that increasing prior experience increases the degree to which current stimuli are "filtered" through this experience and thereby constrained by the consistencies learned in the "real world." This pattern of increasingly constrained learning does not depend on having slow- and fast-learning connections. Other mechanisms of avoiding catastrophic interference, for instance, through the use of reverberated pseudopatterns (Ans, Rousset, French, & Musca, 2004), would generate similar behavior in the network, but possibly at the cost of being less neurally plausible than mechanisms based on slow- and fast-learning units.

EXPERIENCE-DEPENDENT LEARNING

While networks representing the older infants received more training before the habituation phase—and as Simulations 4 and 5 show—different degrees of prior exposure selectively shaped future learning—the architectural parameters for the different networks were extrinsic to the system. That is, the weight-decay and the number of hidden units were manually set to the values in Tables 7 and 8. This contrasts with the "experience-dependent learning" account in which the changes to the learning system are caused by the learning process itself (e.g., Johnson & Munakata, 2005; Munakata & McClelland, 2003). In such a framework, processes like entrenchment play a key role. The difficulty in learning a second language (L2) later in life, for instance, is explained not by the closing of a critical or sensitive language-acquiring period but by the increased entrenchment of the first language (L1). As L1 becomes over-practiced with time, the learning of L2 is progressively made more difficult due to interference from L1 (Seidenberg & Zevin, 2005). The ability of connectionist models to model developmental trajectories in such tasks as object permanence (Munakata, McClelland, Johnson, & Siegler, 1997) and the A-not-B error (Munakata, 1998) with development simply a product of greater experience has raised questions about the need to posit mechanisms that change "simply as a by-product of some autonomous process driven simply by the passage of time" (Munakata & McClelland, 2003, p. 421) and has brought into question the need for such mechanisms.

The idea that architectural changes are caused by the learning process itself is compatible with the CAAL framework. While currently extrinsic, the architectural changes made to the model with development can, in theory, be made intrinsic by introducing mechanisms such as those used in generative architectures (e.g., Mareschal & Schultz, 1996) which recruit new units or connections into the network as a function of experience. In practice, such implementations would need to make multiple assumptions about the nature of neural development—for example, how new units are recruited and integrated into an already-trained network, how existing weights constrain new connectivity patterns—necessary assumptions that call into question the assumed benefit of such generative architectures.

THE ROLE OF LABELING IN EARLY CONCEPTS

A prediction that emerges from our theoretical framework concerns how infants may initially map labels onto moving objects or the features of those objects. Recall that according to our framework, labels are a dynamic feature of objects and the same associative mechanism involved in encoding the static and dynamic visual features of objects should also encode labels into existing representations. In light of previous work that examined infants' attention to relations among dynamic cues (Rakison, 2004; Rakison & Poulin-Dubois, 2002), we expected that when infants are presented with a novel label and an object with dynamic parts that moves—and where the movement is a predictor of category membership—they will associate the word with the dynamic parts of the object. This prediction was borne out by the model as well as by empirical data with infants. However, Simulation 3 and Experiment 1 also revealed that when global motion is not predictive feature of category membership, networks and infants associate labels with static features (e.g., the bodies of objects). Taken together, this suggests that when infants and toddlers hear a novel label in the presence of a global motion they may generalize that label on the basis of dynamic features rather than on the basis of shape (e.g., Smith et al., 1996, 2002).

Although we believe the same general mechanism is involved the development of word learning and object representation, our claim is not that labels are just one more feature of an object. We suggested that labels hold a "privileged status" of sorts, but this is not due to a predisposition to acquire language in the form of a specialized learning mechanism. Instead, in our view labels are dynamic, a perfect predictor of category membership, comprise the type of stimuli that systematically refer to categories (Colunga & Smith, 2002), and do not have to compete with other features for limited attention resources.

In addition, in contrast to other object features a basic-level label such as dog or car is unique to an object category. Because such labels apply to multiple exemplars, learning to associate a label like "dog" with multiple individual dogs results in infants discovering the properties that are consistent across the exemplars and then to associate those properties with the labels (Smith et al., 2002). For example, each time the label "dog" is heard in the presence of a dog, infants observe that the labeled object has four legs, eyes, a head, moves along a specific motion path, and so on. Over time, labels become associated with a whole host of features that are common to members of the category, and the production of the label incites activation of these features. Activating the label in this context facilitates the inference process by activating correlated yet unobserved properties of a labeled object. It is also worth noting that language development more generally may play a crucial role in the emergence of more abstract, accessible concepts. That is, once infants learn a label for a category, associations among features are representationally drawn together under one word, which causes knowledge that was perceptual and procedural to become conceptual and declarative (Rakison, in press).

We believe that the referential property of labels comes from this association of a label with multiple category exemplars. Because the label is shared between category exemplars and is a perfect predictor of the category (e.g., not all dogs are brown, but all dogs are "dogs"), learning labels for categories results in more compact and robust category representations than learning categories using their perceptual features alone (Lupyan, Rakison, & McClelland, 2007), especially when learning categories with large within-category variance and fuzzy boundaries (Lupyan, 2005). While perceptual information for such categories is unreliable, relying on labels as markers of category membership can bootstrap category formation in the face of complex and unreliable perceptual features. It is because labels are perceptually salient (Sloutsky & Napolitano, 2003) and so well correlated with category membership that they can act as "invitations to categories" (Waxman, 2003).

POTENTIAL CRITICISMS OF THE FRAMEWORK

As with any theoretical model of development, our framework is open to a number of potential criticisms. We highlight and address a number of these criticisms in this section. First, as outlined in Chapter I our theoretical perspective is much aligned with that of Eimas and Quinn (1997), Smith and colleagues (e.g., Colunga & Smith, 2005; Jones and Smith, 1993) and Oakes and Madole (1999, 2003). One potential criticism, then, is that our framework is offering nothing new to the already rich literature on concept development. We are not the first, for example, to propose that fundamental mechanism for learning is domain general, that representations are augmented continuously over developmental time, that infants possess a number of inherent attention biases, or that development results from advances in information-processing abilities and neurological maturation. We are also not the first to present a connectionist model of concept development. For example, Mareschal and colleagues (Mareschal, Quinn, & French, 2002; French et al., 2004) have presented a PDP model early concept learning that shows that infants' ability to learn about static features of basic-level categories such as *dog* and *cat* can be explained by bottom-up associative processes, and are dependent on the nature of the stimuli. In our opinion, however, the framework presented here goes beyond these previous formulations because it tackles the more thorny problem of how the infant incorporates static and dynamic features to create concepts that differentiate animates from inanimates. Moreover, we have attempted to describe and explain the mechanisms of change that may be involved in this process, and as such the framework can be related to developmental changes in the broader domain of early conceptual acquisition.

Second, a related potential criticism is that theory and simulations presented here do not refute more nativist views of concept acquisition (e.g., Baillargeon, 2004; Leslie, 1995; Mandler, 1992; Premack, 1990; Spelke, 2004). According to these views, infants possess core principles, specialized mechanisms, or innate modules that facilitate concept acquisition in the first years of life, and it could be argued that we have not provided evidence to the contrary. Our goal in the present work was not to show that these perspectives are inaccurate explanations of concept development; as we discussed earlier we are hesitant as to whether such nativist theoretical perspectives are indeed testable. The model presented here does show, however, that an associative learning mechanism with relatively few built-in assumptions is adequate to explain how and when infants learn about the static and dynamic features typical of animates and inanimates.

Third, although the model was designed to be somewhat neurally plausible—in that there are fast- and slow-learning connections, for example—there are a number of other ways in which the network could have been implemented. We do not make strong claims here about whether our implementation is the only appropriate way in which to model the behavioral data; it is quite possible that models that are grounded more in research from vision science and neuroscience could provide a more veridical implementation. For instance one might explore the implications of the development of ventral and dorsal visual streams (i.e., the "what" and "where" pathways) for learning to form concepts that rely on combinations of static and dynamic features. Our implementation did draw on a number of aspects of developmental cognitive neuroscience—in particular in explaining mechanisms for developmental change—but our goal was focused more on a cognitive model of concept development that a cognitive neuroscience model of concept development. With the current burgeoning interest and advancements in developmental neuroscience, we envisage that it will not be long before more neurologically credible models are realized.

Fourth, because most models use free parameters, there is a concern that a model may be able to fit essentially any data—both observed and unobserved. Fitting such a model to existing data therefore is not a strong test of the theory advocated by the model (Roberts & Pashler, 2000). It is true that as with any model with free parameters, results depend on the choice of parameter values. We have taken every effort to make the values of the theoretically relevant parameters plausible and keep them consistent across simulations. For several simulations, we have tested other values of parameters in an effort to show that the qualitative pattern of the results does not depend on having all the parameters set in a highly particular way. This criticism of data fitting (Roberts & Pashler, 2000) applies most strongly to models whose main claim is their ability to fit existing human data. Our model goes beyond data fitting by making a novel prediction concerning learning the association of labels with dynamic features (Chapter V)— a prediction that has been confirmed by experimental results.

Fifth, we acknowledge the general criticism of connectionist models as being too powerful. It has been claimed that while humans demonstrate clear limits and constraints on learning, connectionist networks are able to learn essentially any pattern of inputs (Massaro, 1988). The constraints we have implemented in the current model show that inherent biases (e.g., a preference for attending to moving stimuli) combined with observation of certain correlations before habituation can generate expectations that guide and constrain future learning. Nevertheless, the present model does not fully address Massaro's criticism. The architecture of our model is indeed flexible enough to demonstrate learning not attested to in infants. Specifically, though pretraining creates certain biases, a sufficient amount of subsequent training can nevertheless override them. Future models can explore more fully the conceptual domains in which inherent biases and prior experience result in entrenchment of the learning system, and which domains are more flexible and can be superseded by experience (see Regier, 2003a, 2003b, for excellent discussions of modeling constraints).

The simulations and experiments reported here represent a first step in corroborating an associative learning framework for early object concept development. The data thus far support the notion that CAAL can account for how and when infants learn about three of the motion characteristics outlined by Rakison and Poulin-Dubois (2001); yet it is imperative to assess whether the model can account for early learning of the other motion characteristics of animates and inanimates. The same simple Michotte-like events employed here are suitable to examine infants' ability to encode form of causal action (action at a distance vs. caused motion) and pattern of interaction (contingent vs. noncontingent). One clear prediction of our model is that learning for these motions will exhibit the same developmental trend as that observed by Rakison (2005a, 2006) and replicated in Simulations 4 and 5. Our framework is applicable also to goal-directed action—motion that is targeted at another referent in the world—which is specified entirely in the perceptual input. Indeed, we view our domain-general theoretical perspective as compatible with that of Woodward (1998, 1999; Woodward, Sommerville, & Guajardo, 2001) who suggested that infants' interpretation of action as goal directed is tightly initially connected to the surface characteristics of hands. That is, infants first identify as goal directed certain actions that they themselves produced or observed, with hands being associatively related to these actions.

Although the simulations and experiments reported here focused on the habituation paradigm in which novel stimuli were used, CAAL makes specific predictions about the way in which infants will categorize and make inductive generalizations about real-world objects. One clear prediction of the framework is that infants will initially categorize objects such as animals and vehicles on the basis of their surface features involved in motion—legs and wheels, for example—rather than on the basis of category relations or "animacy." Similarly, it is predicted that the basis for early induction will be the features that are associated with specific motions. Evidence to support both of these predictions was found using distinct experimental paradigm with 18-month-old infants: Using the sequential touching procedure it was shown that they rely on object parts such as legs and wheels to categorize at the superordinate and basic level (Rakison & Butterworth, 1998; Rakison & Cohen, 1999), and using the inductive generalization procedure it was shown that they generalize motion properties such as "walking" and "rolling" on the basis of those parts (Rakison, 2005b). Further research is necessary to confirm whether, as predicted by CAAL, infants associate the parts of a real-world object with motion characteristics such as agency and self-propulsion as well as other actions that are typical of animates and inanimates (e.g., mouths associated with eating). Research is already underway with the inductive generalization procedure to test infants' generalization of goal-directed action to animals and not vehicles and has thus far yielded positive results (Cicchino & Rakison, 2007).

The framework presented here makes also specific predictions about the role of labels on early concept development. Some of these predictions were borne out by the simulations and experiments with 18-month-old infants, but additional research is required to corroborate these findings. In particular, it is important to show that infants will initially generalize labels for real objects—not those presented on a computer screen—on the basis of parts rather than shape and that this occurs when global motion is present to act as a facilitating cue. Previous work using simpler, feed-forward neural networks made predictions regarding category variance, in particular that associating basic-level labels with category members is more useful in learning categories with large internal variance (Lupyan, 2005). For instance, the category of actions associated with a verb like "walk" encompasses a large degree of perceptual variability. Further empirical work needs to be done to determine what role, if any, verbal labels play in the formation of such categories.

The model of CAAL described here provides an implementations of all six fundamental features of the framework as presented in the introduction. The theoretical account, however, includes elements not explicitly tested. For instance, among inherent perceptual biases we mentioned is a bias to attend to larger rather than smaller features. Though not tested here, this is an assumption that emerges naturally from connectionist architectures —features that span across more units contribute more to the network error and so participate more in guiding the learning process than features represented with fewer units in the input. We recognize that the implementation of development as an increase in the number of fast-learning hidden units, combined with a progressively lower weight-decay rate, is a gross simplification of neural development. Future, more detailed, models can make closer contact with the neuroscience literature and make specific predictions about the impact of the neural development of such as the hippocampus on the learning of conceptual relations.

In all the simulations reported here, the models were trained on patterns corresponding to perceptual features. It is possible, however, to train the model on concept representations automatically derived from linguistic contexts in which words occur (Rohde et al., 2007). Studying the representations formed in networks trained on such patterns offers another avenue for examining the emergence of learning constraints and general-ization behavior. Because (1) animate concepts cluster with other animates, and inanimate concepts cluster with other inanimates; (2) causal events are more likely to have animate agents and inanimate recipients than noncausal events; and (3) noncausal events are more likely to have animate

97

(i.e., self-propelled) "recipients," a network trained on causal and noncausal "scenes" can generalize to novel scenes and predict whether these scenes display causal or noncausal relations (Lupyan & Rakison, 2006). We do not deny that generalization is strongly determined by context. For instance, Opfer and Bullock (2006) found that preschool-age children generalized based on similarity in a noncausal context but generalized based on origin information when presented with information about biological origin of the stimuli. Because internal representations in connectionist models are highly dimensional, similarity space is a function of context (Rogers & McClelland, 2004). Examining the role of context in networks trained on richer inputs under various contexts is likely to lead to more ecologically valid models of concept development in infancy and beyond.

CONCLUSIONS

We have offered a new framework—called constrained attentional associative learning or CAAL (Rakison, 2005a, 2006)—that has at its core the notion that general rather than specific mechanisms underpin early object concept development. We presented a model, simulations, and novel experimental evidence that support the view that associative processes are the fundamental mechanism for learning, that representations are continuously augmented over developmental time, that infants possess a number of inherent attention biases, and that development in this domain is propelled by advances in information-processing abilities.

To conclude we return to a point that was made in Chapter I. The model, simulations, and experiments detailed here, as would be the case for any attempt to provide such a framework, present a *sufficiency account* for early concept development. At this point in time the experimental techniques do not exist that allow theorists to test whether their model is a veridical depiction of how development occurs in infants and young children. At the same time, however, there is now an abundance of evidence that supports the model outlined here, and the computational approach we have adopted offers a way in which theoretical assumptions about the nature of development can be tested. We believe that this dual approach represents the way forward and will ultimately prove fruitful in the continuing quest to elucidate the origins, nature, and development of knowledge.

INPUT–OUTPUT PAIRS USED IN TRAINING OF THE MOVING-PARTS CONDITIONS
IN SIMULATION 1

Object 1:

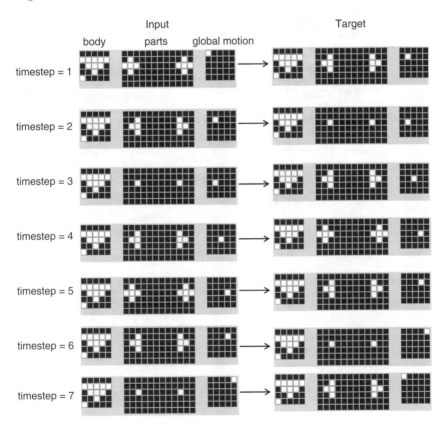

Object 2:

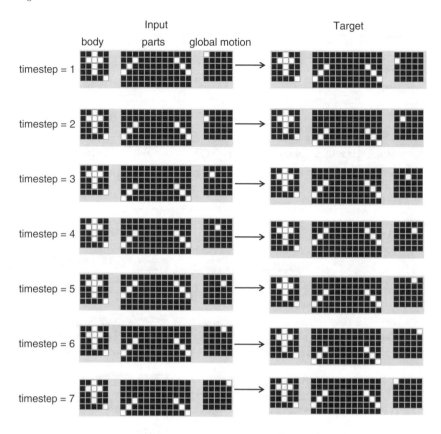

REFERENCES

Ans, B., Rousset, S., French, R. M., & Musca, S. (2004). Self-refreshing memory in artificial neural networks: Learning temporal sequences without catastrophic forgetting. *Connection Science*, **16**, 71–99.

Arterberry, M. E. (1993). Development of spatiotemporal integration in infancy. *Infant Behavior and Development*, **16**, 343–363.

Arterberry, M. E., & Bornstein, M. H. (2002). Infant perceptual and conceptual categorization: The roles of static and dynamic stimulus attributes. *Cognition*, **86**, 1–24.

Baillargeon, R. (1995). Physical reasoning in infancy. In M. S. Gazzaniga (Ed.), *The cognitive neurosciences* (pp. 181–204). Cambridge, MA: MIT Press.

Baillargeon, R. (1998). Infants' understanding of the physical world. In M. Sabourin, F. Craik & M. Robert (Eds.), *Advances in psychological science: Vol. 2. Biological and cognitive aspects* (pp. 503–529). East Sussex, U.K.: Psychology Press.

Baillargeon, R. (1999). Young infants' expectations about hidden objects: A reply to three challenges. *Developmental Science*, **2**, 115–132.

Baillargeon, R. (2001). Infants' physical knowledge: Of acquired expectations and core principles. In E. Dupoux (Ed.), *Language, brain, and cognitive development: Essays in honor of Jacques Mehler* (pp. 341–361). Cambridge, MA: The MIT Press.

Baillargeon, R. (2004). Infants' physical world. *Current Directions in Psychological Science*, **13**, 89–94.

Baillargeon, R., Kotovsky, L., & Needham, A. (1995). The acquisition of physical knowledge in infancy. In D. Sperber, D. Premack & A. J. Premack (Eds.), *Causal cognition: A multidisciplinary debate* (pp. 79–116). New York, NY: Oxford University Press.

Bakeman, R., & Adamson, L. B. (1984). Coordinating attention to people and objects in mother–infant and peer–infant interaction. *Child Development*, **55**, 1278–1289.

Baldi, P., & Hornik, K. (1989). Neural networks and principal component analysis—learning from examples without local minima. *Neural Networks*, **2**, 53–58.

Baldwin, D. A., Baird, J. A., Saylor, M. M., & Clark, M. A. (2001). Infants parse dynamic action. *Child Development*, **72**, 708–717.

Bauer, P. J. (2006). Constructing a past in infancy: A neuro-developmental account. *Trends Cognitive Sciences*, **10**, 175–181.

Behl-Chadha, G. (1996). Basic-level and superordinate-like categorical representations in early infancy. *Cognition*, **60**, 105–141.

Carey, S. (1985). *Conceptual change in childhood*. Cambridge, MA: MIT Press.

Chao, L. L., & Martin, A. (2000). Representation of manipulable man-made objects in the dorsal stream. *NeuroImage*, **12**, 478–484.

Chaput, H. H., & Cohen, L. B. (2001). A model of infant causal perception and its development. In J. D. Moore & K. Stenning (Eds.), *Proceedings of the Twenty-Third Annual Conference of the Cognitive Science Society* (pp. 182–187). Mahwah, NJ: Erlbaum.

Cicchino, J. B., & Rakison, D. H. (2007). *Infants' attribution of goal-directed action to non-human animals.* Manuscript under review.

Clark, A. (1997). *Being there: Putting brain, body and world together again.* Cambridge, MA: MIT Press.

Cohen, L. B., & Menten, T. G. (1981). The rise and fall of infant habituation. *Infant Behavior and Development*, **4**, 269–280.

Cohen, L. B., & Oakes, L. M. (1993). How infants perceive a simple causal event. *Developmental Psychology*, **29**, 421–433.

Columbo, J. (1993). *Infant cognition: Predicting later intellectual functioning.* Newbury Park, CA: Sage.

Columbo, J. (1995). On the neural mechanisms underlying developmental and individual differences in visual fixation in infancy: Two hypotheses. *Developmental Review*, **15**, 97–135.

Colunga, E., & Smith, L. B. (2002). What makes a word? In W. D. Gray & C. D. Schunn (Eds.), *Proceedings of the Annual Conference of the Cognitive Science Society* (Vol. 24, pp. 214–219). Mahwah, NJ: Erlbaum.

Colunga, E., & Smith, L. B. (2005). From the lexicon to expectations about kinds: A role for associative learning. *Psychological Review*, **112**, 347–382.

Diamond, A. (1991). Neuropsychological insights into the meaning of object concept development. In S. Carey & R. Gelman (Eds.), *The epigenesis of mind: Essays on biology and cognition* (pp. 67–110). Hillsdale, NJ: Erlbaum.

Eimas, P. D. (1994). Categorization in infancy and the continuity of development. *Cognition*, **50**, 83–93.

Eimas, P. D., & Quinn, P. C. (1994). Studies on the formation of perceptually based basic-level categories in young infants. *Child Development*, **65**, 903–917.

Elman, J. L. (1990). Finding structure in time. *Cognitive Science*, **14**, 179–211.

Fiser, J., & Aslin, R. N. (2001). Unsupervised statistical learning of higher-order spatial structures from visual scenes. *Psychological Science*, **12**, 499–504.

Fiser, J., & Aslin, R. N. (2002). Statistical learning of new visual feature combinations by infants. *Proceedings of the National Academy of Sciences*, **99**, 15822–15826.

Földiák, P. (1998). Learning constancies for object perception. In V. Walsh & J. J. Kulikowski (Eds.), *Perceptual constancy: Why things look as they do* (pp. 144–172). Cambridge, U.K.: Cambridge University Press.

French, R. M., Mareschal, D., Mermillod, M., & Quinn, P. C. (2004). The role of bottom-up processing in perceptual categorization by 3- to 4-month-old infants: Simulations and data. *Journal of Experimental Psychology: General*, **133**, 382–397.

Gelman, R. (1990). First principles organize attention to and learning about relevant data: Number and the animate–inanimate distinction as examples. *Cognitive Science*, **14**, 79–106.

Gelman, R., Durgin, F., & Kaufman, L. (1995). Distinguishing between animate and inanimates: Not by motion alone. In D. Sperber, D. Premack & A. J. Premack (Eds.), *Causal cognition* (pp. 150–184). Oxford, U.K.: Clarendon.

Gelman, R., & Spelke, E. S. (1981). The development of thoughts about animate and inanimate objects: Implications for research on social cognition. In J. H. Flavell & L. Ross (Eds.), *Social cognition* (pp. 43–66). New York: Academic.

Gibson, J. J. (1966). *The senses considered as a perceptual system.* New York: Houghton Mifflin.

Gilmore, R. O., & Thomas, H. (2002). Examining individual differences in infants' habituation patterns using objectives quantitative techniques. *Infant Behavior and Development*, **25**, 399–412.

Gogate, L. J., & Bahrick, L. E. (1998). Intersensory redundancy facilitates learning of arbitrary relations between vowel sounds and objects in seven-month-old infants. *Journal of Experimental Child Psychology*, **69**, 133–149.

Goldman-Rakic, P. S. (1987). Circuitry of primate prefrontal cortex and regulation of behavior by representational memory. In F. Plum (Ed.), *Handbook of physiology, the nervous system, higher functions of the brain* (Vol. 5, pp. 373–417). Bethesda, MD: American Physiological Society.

Granrud, C. E. (1993). *Visual perception and cognition in infancy*. Hillsdale, NJ: Erlbaum.

Gureckis, T. M., & Love, B. C. (2004). Common mechanisms in infant and adult category learning. *Infancy*, **5**, 173–198.

Haith, M. M. (1998). Who put the cog in infant cognition? Is rich interpretation too costly? *Infant Behavior and Development*, **21**, 167–179.

Hayne, H. (1996). Categorization in infancy. In C. Rovee-Collier & L. P. Lipsitt (Eds.), *Advances in infancy research* (Vol. 10, pp. 79–120). Norwood, NJ: Ablex.

Hinton, G. E., & Plaut, D. C. (1987). Using fast weights to deblur old memories. In *Proceedings of the 9th Annual Conference of the Cognitive Science Society* (pp. 177–186). Hillsdale, NJ: Lawrence Erlbaum Associates.

Hintzman, D. L. (1991). Why are formal models useful in psychology? In E. W. Hockley & S. Lewandowsky (Eds.), *Relating theory and data: Essays on human memory in honor of Bennet B. Murdock* (pp. 39–56). Hillsdale, NJ: Lawrence Erlbaum Associates Inc.

Horst, J. S., Oakes, L. M., & Madole, K. L. (2005). What does it look like and what can it do? Category structure influences how infants categorize. *Child Development*, **76**, 614–631.

Houston, D. M., & Jusczyk, P. W. (2000). The role of talker-specific information in word segmentation by infants. *Journal of Experimental Psychology: Human Perception and Performance*, **26**, 1570–1582.

Huttenlocher, P. R., & Dabholkar, A. S. (1997). Regional differences in synaptogenesis in human cerebral cortex. *Journal of Computational Neuroscience*, **387**, 167–178.

Japkowicz, N., Hanson, S. J., & Gluck, M. A. (2000). Nonlinear autoassociation is not equivalent to PCA. *Neural Computation*, **12**, 531–545.

Johnson, M. H. (1990). Cortical maturation and the development of visual attention in early infancy. *Journal of Cognitive Neuroscience*, **2**, 81–95.

Johnson, M. H., & Morton, J. (1991). *Biology and cognitive development: The case for face recognition*. Oxford: Basil Blackwell Limited.

Johnson, M. H., & Munakata, Y. (2005). Processes of change in brain and cognitive development. *Trends in Cognitive Sciences*, **9**, 152–158.

Jones, S. S., & Smith, L. B. (1993). The place of perception in children's concepts. *Cognitive Development*, **8**, 113–139.

Kagan, J., McCall, R. B., Reppucci, N. D., Jordan, J., Levine, J., & Minton, C. (1971). *Change and continuity in infancy*. New York: Wiley.

Kaldy, Z., Blaser, E., & Leslie, A. M. (2006). A new method for calibrating perceptual salience across dimensions in infants: The case of color vs. luminance. *Developmental Science*, **9**, 482–489.

Kaldy, Z., & Leslie, A. M. (2003). Identification of objects in 9-month-old infants: Integrating "what" and "where" information. *Developmental Science*, **6**, 360–373.

Kaldy, Z., & Sigala, N. (2004). The neural mechanisms of object working memory: What is where in the infant brain? *Neuroscience and Biobehavioral Reviews*, **28**, 113–121.

Kanazawa, S., Shira, N., Ohtsuka, Y., & Yamaguchi, M. K. (2006). Perception of opposite-moving dots in 3- to 5-month-old infants. *Vision Research*, **46**, 346–356.

Kaplan, P. S., & Werner, J. S. (1986). Habituation, response to novelty, and dishabituation in human infants: Tests of a dual-process theory of visual attention. *Journal of Experimental Child Psychology*, **42**, 199–217.

Keil, F. C. (1981). Constraints on knowledge and cognitive development. *Psychological Review*, **88**, 197–227.

Kirkham, N. Z., Slemmer, J. A., & Johnson, S. P. (2002). Visual statistical learning in infancy: Evidence of a domain general learning mechanism. *Cognition*, **83**, 35–42.

Kuhlmeier, V. A., Bloom, P., & Wynn, K. (2004). Do 5-month-old infants see humans as material objects? *Cognition*, **94**, 95–103.

Leslie, A. (1994). ToMM, ToBy, and Agency: Core architecture and domain specificity. In L. Hirschfeld & S. Gelman (Eds.), *Mapping the mind: Domain specificity in cognition and culture* (pp. 119–148). New York: Cambridge University Press.

Leslie, A. (1995). A theory of agency. In D. Sperber, D. Premack & A. J. Premack (Eds.), *Causal cognition* (pp. 121–141). Oxford: Clarendon.

Leslie, A. M., & Keeble, S. (1987). Do six-month-old infants perceive causality? *Cognition*, **25**, 265–288.

Lewis, T. L., Maurer, D., & Brent, H. P. (1989). Optokinetic nystagmus in normal and visually deprived children: Implications for cortical development. *Canadian Journal of Psychology*, **43**, 121–140.

Lund, K., & Burgess, C. (1996). Producing high-dimensional semantic spaces from lexical co-occurrence. *Behavior Research Methods, Instruments, and Computers*, **28**, 203–208.

Luo, Y., & Baillargeon, R. (2005). Can a self-propelled box have a goal? Psychological reasoning in 5-month-old infants. *Psychological Science*, **16**, 601–608.

Lupyan, G. (2005). Carving nature at its joints and carving joints into nature: How labels augment category representations. In A. Cangelosi, G. Bugmann & R. Borisyuk (Eds.), *Modelling language, cognition and action: Proceedings of the 9th Neural Computation and Psychology Workshop* (pp. 87–96). Singapore: World Scientific.

Lupyan, G., & Rakison, D. H. (2006). What moves in a mysterious way? A domain-general account of learning about animacy and causality. In R. Sun & N. Miyake (Eds.), *The 28th Annual Conference of the Cognitive Science Society* (pp. 525–530). Mahwah, NJ: Erlbaum.

Lupyan, Rakison, D. H., & McClelland, J. L. (2007). Language is not just for talking: Redundant labels facilitate learning of novel categories. *Psychological Science*, **18**, 1077–1083.

Madole, K. L., & Cohen, L. B. (1995). The role of object parts in infants' attention to form–function correlations. *Developmental Psychology*, **31**, 637–648.

Madole, K. L., & Oakes, L. M. (1999). Making sense of infant categorization: Stable processes and changing representations. *Developmental Review*, **19**, 263–296.

Madole, K. L., Oakes, L. M., & Cohen, L. B. (1993). Developmental changes in infants' attention to function and form-function correlations. *Cognitive Development*, **8**, 189–209.

Mandler, J. M. (1992). How to build a baby II. Conceptual primitives. *Psychological Review*, **99**, 587–604.

Mandler, J. M. (2000). Perceptual and conceptual processes in infancy. *Journal of Cognition and Development*, **1**, 3–36.

Mandler, J. M. (2003). Conceptual categorization. In D. H. Rakison & L. M. Oakes (Eds.), *Early category and concept development: Making sense of the blooming, buzzing confusion* (pp. 103–131). New York: Oxford University Press.

Mandler, J. M., Bauer, P. J., & McDonough, L. (1991). Separating the sheep from the goats: Differentiating global categories. *Cognitive Psychology*, **23**, 263–298.

Mandler, J. M., & McDonough, L. (1993). Concept formation in infancy. *Cognitive Development*, **8**, 291–318.

Mandler, J. M., & McDonough, L. (1996). Drinking and driving don't mix: Inductive generalization in infancy. *Cognition*, **59**, 307–335.

Mandler, J. M., & McDonough, L. (1998). Studies in inductive inference in infancy. *Cognitive Psychology*, **37**, 60–96.

Mareschal, D. (2003). The acquisition of use of implicit categories in early development. In D. H. Rakison & L. M. Oakes (Eds.), *Early category and concept development: Making sense of the blooming, buzzing confusion* (pp. 360–383). New York: Oxford University Press.

Mareschal, D., & Shultz, T. R. (1996). Generative connectionist networks and constructivist cognitive development. *Cognitive Development*, **11**, 571–603.

Mareschal, D., Quinn, P. C., & French, R. M. (2002). Asymmetric interference in 3- to 4-month olds' sequential category learning. *Cognitive Science*, **26**, 377–389.

Markman, E. M. (1989). *Categorization and naming in children: Problems of induction*. Cambridge, MA: MIT Press.

Markson, L., & Spelke, E. S. (2006). Infants' rapid learning about self-propelled objects. *Infancy*, **9**, 45–71.

Massaro, D. (1988). Some criticisms of connectionist models of human performance. *Journal of Memory and Language*, **27**, 213–234.

McClelland, J. L. (1988). Connectionist models and psychological evidence. *Journal of Memory and Language*, **27**, 107–123.

McClelland, J. L., McNaughton, B. L., & O'Reilly, R. C. (1995). Why there are complementary learning systems in hippocampus and neocortex: Insights from the successes and failures of connectionist models of learning and memory. *Psychological Review*, **102**, 419–457.

McCloskey, M., & Cohen, N. J. (1989). Catastrophic interference in connectionist networks: The sequential learning problem. *The Psychology of Learning and Motivation*, **24**, 109–165.

McRae, K., Cree, G. S., Seidenberg, M. S., & McNorgan, C. (2005). Semantic feature production norms for a large set of living and nonliving things. *Behavioral Research Methods, Instrumentation, and Computers*, **37**, 547–559.

Meltzoff, A. N. (1990). Towards a developmental cognitive science: The implications of cross-modal matching and imitation for the development of representation and memory in infancy. In A. Diamond (Ed.), *The development and neural bases of higher cognitive functions, Annals of the New York Academy of Sciences* (Vol. 608, pp. 1–31). New York: New York Academy of Sciences.

Milner, D., & Goodale, M. A. (1995). *The visual brain in action*. New York, NY: Oxford University Press.

Munakata, Y. (1998). Infant perseveration and implications for object permanence theories: A PDP Model of the a_b task. *Developmental Science*, **1**, 161–184.

Munakata, Y. (2006). Information processing approaches to development. In W. Damon & R. Lerner (Series Eds.), D. Kuhn & R. S. Siegler (Vol. Eds.), *Handbook of child psychology: Vol. 2: Cognition, perception, and language* (6th ed., pp. 426–463). New York: Wiley.

Munakata, Y., & McClelland, J. L. (2003). Connectionist models of development. *Developmental Science*, **6**, 413–429.

Munakata, Y., McClelland, J. L., Johnson, M. H., & Siegler, R. S. (1997). Rethinking infant knowledge: Toward an adaptive process account of successes and failures in object permanence tasks. *Psychological Review*, **104**, 686–713.

Murphy, G. L. (2002). *The big book of concepts*. Cambridge, MA: MIT Press.

Namy, L., Campbell, A., & Tomasello, M. (2004). Developmental change in the role of iconicity in symbol learning. *Journal of Cognition and Development*, **5**, 37–57.

Namy, L. L., & Waxman, S. R. (1998). Words and gestures: Infants' interpretations of different forms of symbolic reference. *Child Development*, **69**, 295–308.

Nelson, K. (1973). Some evidence for the cognitive primacy of categorization and its functional basis. *Merrill-Palmer Quarterly*, **19**, 21–39.

Oakes, L. M., & Cohen, L. B. (1990). Infant perception of a causal event. *Cognitive Development*, **5**, 193–207.

Oakes, L. M., & Madole, K. L. (2003). Principles of developmental change in infants' category formation. In D. H. Rakison & L. M. Oakes (Eds.), *Early category and concept development: Making sense of the blooming, buzzing confusion* (pp. 159–192). New York: Oxford University Press.

Oakes, L. M., Ross-Sheehy, S., & Luck, S. J. (2006). Rapid development of feature binding in visual short-term memory. *Psychological Science*, **17**, 781–787.

Opfer, J. E., & Bulloch, M. J. (2007). Causal relations drive young children's induction, naming, and categorization. *Cognition*, **105**, 206–217.

Pauen, S. (2002). Evidence for knowledge-based category discrimination in infancy. *Child Development*, **73**, 1016–1033.

Perone, S., & Oakes, L. M. (2006). It clicks when it is rolled and it squeaks when it is squeezed: What 10-month-old infants learn about object function. *Child Development*, **77**, 1608–1622.

Piaget, J. (1952). *The origins of intelligence in the childhood.* New York: International Universities Press.

Premack, D. (1990). The infants' theory of self-propelled objects. *Cognition*, **36**, 1–16.

Pulverman, R., Hirsh-Pasek, K., Pruden, S., & Golinkoff, R. (2006). Precursors to verb learning: Infant attention to manner and path. *Fruhforderung Interdisziplinar*, **25**, 3–13.

Quinn, P. C., & Eimas, P. D. (1996). Perceptual organization and categorization. In C. Rovee-Collier & L. Lipsitt (Eds.), *Advances in infancy research* (Vol. 10, pp. 1–36). Norwood, NJ: Ablex Publishing.

Quinn, P. C., & Eimas, P. D. (1997). A reexamination of the perceptual-to-conceptual shift in mental representations. *Review of General Psychology*, **1**, 171–187.

Quinn, P. C., & Eimas, P. D. (2000). The emergence of category representations during infancy: Are separate perceptual and conceptual processes required? *Journal of Cognition and Development*, **1**, 55–61.

Quinn, P. C., Eimas, P. D., & Rosenkrantz, S. L. (1993). Evidence for representations of perceptually similar natural categories by 3-month-old and 4-month-old infants. *Perception*, **22**, 463–475.

Quinn, P. C., Johnson, M., Mareschal, D., Rakison, D., & Younger, B. (2000). Response to Mandler and Smith: A dual process framework for understanding early categorization? *Infancy*, **1**, 111–122.

Rakison, D. H. (2003). Parts, categorization, and the animate–inanimate distinction in infancy. In D. H. Rakison & L. M. Oakes (Eds.), *Early category and concept development: Making sense of the blooming buzzing confusion* (pp. 159–192). New York, NY: Oxford University Press.

Rakison, D. H. (2004). Infants' sensitivity to correlations among static and dynamic features in a category context. *Journal of Experimental Child Psychology*, **89**, 1–30.

Rakison, D. H. (2005a). A secret agent? How infants learn about the identity of objects in a causal scene. *Journal of Experimental Child Psychology*, **91**, 271–296.

Rakison, D. H. (2005b). Developing knowledge of motion properties in infancy. *Cognition*, **96**, 183–214.

Rakison, D. H. (2006). Make the first move: How infants learn about the identity of self-propelled objects. *Developmental Psychology*, **42**, 900–912.

Rakison, D. H. (2007). Is consciousness in its infancy in infancy? *Journal of Consciousness Studies*, **14**, 66–89.

Rakison, D. H., & Butterworth, G. (1998a). Infants' use of parts in early categorization. *Developmental Psychology*, **34**, 49–62.

Rakison, D. H., & Cohen, L. B. (1999). Infants' use of functional parts in basic-like categorization. *Developmental Science*, **2**, 423–432.

Rakison, D. H., & Hahn, E. (2004). The mechanisms of early categorization and induction: Smart or dumb infants? In R. Kail (Ed.), *Advances in child development and behavior* (Vol. 32, pp. 281–322). New York: Academic Press.

Rakison, D. H., & Poulin-Dubois, D. (2001). Developmental origin of the animate–inanimate distinction. *Psychological Bulletin*, **127**, 209–228.

Rakison, D. H., & Poulin-Dubois, D. (2002). You go this way and I'll go that way: Developmental changes in infants' attention to correlations among dynamic parts in motion events. *Child Development*, **73**, 682–699.

Regier, T. (2003a). Constraining computational models of cognition. In L. Nadel (Ed.), *Encyclopedia of cognitive science* (pp. 611–615). London: Macmillan.

Regier, T. (2003b). Emergent constraints on word-learning: A computational review. *Trends in Cognitive Sciences*, **7**, 263–268.

Rogers, T. T., & McClelland, J. L. (2004). *Semantic cognition: A parallel distributed processing approach*. Cambridge, MA: MIT Press.

Roberts, S., & Pashler, H. (2000). How persuasive is a good fit? A comment on theory testing. *Psychological Review*, **107**, 358–367.

Robinson, C. W., & Sloutsky, V. M. (2004). Auditory dominance and its change in the course of development. *Child Development*, **75**, 1387–1401.

Rochat, P. (2001). *The infant's world*. Cambridge: Harvard University Press.

Rohde, D. L. T., Gonnerman, L., & Plaut, D. C. (2007). An improved model of semantic similarity based on lexical co-occurrence. Manuscript under review.

Rogers, T. T., Rakison, D. H., & McClelland, J. M. (2004). U-shaped curves in development: A PDP approach. *Journal of Cognition and Development*, **5**, 137–145.

Rosch, E., & Mervis, C. B. (1975). Family resemblances: Studies in the internal structure of categories. *Cognitive Psychology*, **7**, 573–605.

Rose, S. A., Gottfried, A. W., Melloy-Carminar, P., & Bridger, W. H. (1982). Familiarity and novelty preferences in infant recognition memory: Implications for information processing. *Developmental Psychology*, **18**, 704–713.

Ross-Sheehy, S., Oakes, L. M., & Luck, S. J. (2003). The development of visual short-term memory capacity in infants. *Child Development*, **74**, 1807–1822.

Rovee-Collier, C., & Gerhardstein, P. (1997). The development of infant memory. In N. Cowan (Ed.), *The development of memory in childhood* (pp. 5–39). Hove, U.K.: Psychology Press.

Ruff, H. A., & Rothbart, M. , K. (1996). *Attention in early development: Themes and variations*. New York, NY: Oxford University Press.

Ruff, H. A., & Saltarelli, L. M. (1993). Exploratory play with objects: Basic cognitive processes and individual differences. In M. Bornstein & A. W. O'Reilly (Eds.), *The role of play in the development of thought* (pp. 5–16). San Francisco, CA: Jossey-Bass.

Ruff, H. A., Saltarelli, L. M., Capozzoli, M., & Dubiner, K. (1992). The differentiation of activity in infants' exploration of objects. *Developmental Psychology*, **28**, 851–861.

Rumelhart, D. E., Hinton, G. E., & Williams, R. J. (1986). Learning representations by back-propagating errors. *Nature*, **323**, 533–536.

Saffran, J. R., Aslin, R. N., & Newport, E. L. (1996). Statistical learning by 8-month old infants. *Science*, **274**, 1926–1928.

Salapatek, P. (1975). Pattern perception in early infancy. In L. B. Cohen & P. Salapatek (Eds.), *Infant perception: From sensation to cognition* (Vol. 1, pp. 133–248). New York: Academic Press.

Samuelson, L. K., & Smith, L. B. (1999). Early noun vocabularies: Do ontology, category structure, and syntax correspond. *Cognition*, **73**, 1–33.

Schlesinger, M., & Parisi, D. (2004). Beyond backprop: Emerging trends in connectionist models of development: an introduction. *Developmental Science*, **7**, 131–132.

Seidenberg, M. S., & Zevin, J. D. (2005). Connectionist models in developmental cognitive neuroscience: Critical periods and the paradox of success. In: Y. Munakata & M. Johnson (Eds.), *Attention & performance XXI: Processes of change in brain and cognitive development* (pp. 585–612). New York: Oxford University Press.

Serres, L. (2001). Morphological changes of the human hippocampal formation from mid-gestation to early childhood. In C. A. Nelson & M. Luciana (Eds.), *Handbook of developmental cognitive neuroscience* (pp. 45–58). Cambridge, MA: MIT Press.

Schafer, G., & Mareschal, D. (2001). Modeling infant speech sound discrimination using simple associative networks. *Infancy*, **2**, 7–28.

Siegler, R. S. (1996). *Emerging minds*. New York, NY: Oxford University Press.

Shira, N., Kanazawa, S., & Yamaguchi, M. K. (2006). Anisotropic motion coherence sensitivities to expansion/contraction motion in early infancy. *Infant Behavior and Development*, **29**, 204–209.

Sirois, S., & Mareschal, D. (2002). Models of habituation in infancy. *Trends in Cognitive Sciences*, **6**, 293–298.

Slater, A. M. (1989). Visual memory and perception in early infancy. In A. Slater & G. Bremner (Eds.), *Infant development* (pp. 43–72). Hove, U.K.: Lawrence Erlbaum Associates.

Slater, A. M., Mattock, A., & Brown, E. (1990). Size constancy at birth: Newborn infants' responses to retinal and real size. *Journal of Experimental Child Psychology*, **49**, 314–322.

Slater, A. M., Mattock, A., Brown, E., Burnham, D., & Young, A. W. (1991). Visual processing of stimulus compounds in newborn babies. *Perception*, **20**, 29–33.

Sloutsky, V. M., & Napolitano, A. C. (2003). Is a picture worth a thousand words? Preference for auditory modality in young children. *Child Development*, **74**, 822–833.

Spelke, E. S. (1994). Initial knowledge: Six suggestions. *Cognition*, **50**, 431–445.

Spelke, E. S., Breinlinger, K., Macomber, J., & Jacobson, K. (1992). Origins of knowledge. *Psychological Review*, **99**, 605–632.

Spelke, E. S., & Kinzler, K. D. (2007). Core knowledge. *Developmental Science*, **10**, 89–96.

Spelke, E. S., Phillips, A. T., & Woodward, A. L. (1995). Infants' knowledge of object motion and human action. In D. Sperber, D. Premack & A. Premack (Eds.), *Causal cognition: A multidisciplinary debate* (pp. 44–78). New York, NY: Oxford University Press.

Smith, L. B., Colunga, E., & Yoshida, H. (2003). Making an ontology: Cross-linguistic evidence. In D. H. Rakison & L. M. Oakes (Eds.), *Early category and concept development: Making sense of the blooming buzzing confusion* (pp. 275–302). New York: Oxford University Press.

Smith, L. B., & Heise, D. (1992). Perceptual similarity and conceptual structure. In B. Burns (Ed.), *Percepts, concepts, and categories* (pp. 233–272). Amsterdam: Elsevier.

Smith, L. B., Jones, S. S., & Landau, B. (1996). Naming in young children: A dumb attentional mechanism? *Cognition*, **60**, 143–171.

Smith, L. B., Jones, S. S., Landau, B., Gershkoff-Stowe, L., & Samuelson, S. (2002). Early noun learning provides on-the-job training for attention. *Psychological Science*, **13**, 13–19.

Squire, L. R., Knowlton, B., & Musen, G. (1993). The structure and organization of memory. *Annual Review of Psychology*, **44**, 453–495.

Stager, C. L., & Werker, J. F. (1997). Infants listen for more phonetic detail in speech perception than in word-learning tasks. *Nature*, **388**, 381–382.

Strange, W. (1989). Dynamic specification of coarticulated vowels spoken in sentence context. *Journal of the Acoustical Society of America*, **85**, 2135–2153.

Tenenbaum, J. B., Griffiths, T. L., & Kemp, C. (2006). Theory-based Bayesian models of inductive learning and reasoning. *Trends in Cognitive Sciences*, **10**, 309–318.

Todd, J. J., & Marois, R. (2004). Capacity limit of visual short-term memory in human posterior parietal cortex. *Nature*, **428**, 751–754.

Ungerleider, L. G., & Mishkin, M. (1982). Two cortical visual systems. In D. J. Ingle, M. A. Goodale & R. J. Mansfield (Eds.), *Analysis of visual behavior* (pp. 549–586). Cambridge, MA: MIT Press.

Vallortigara, G., Regolin, L., & Marconato, F. (2005). Visually inexperienced chicks exhibit a spontaneous preference for biological motion patterns. *PLoS Biology*, **3**, 1312–1316.

Wang, S., Baillargeon, R., & Paterson, S. (2005). Detecting continuity violations in infancy: A new account and new evidence from covering and tube events. *Cognition*, **95**, 129–173.

Wattam-Bell, J. (1996). Visual motion processing in one-month-old infants: Habituation experiments. *Vision Research*, **36**, 1679–1685.

Waxman, S. R. (2003). Links between object categorization and naming: Origins and emergence in human infants. In D. H. Rakison & L. M. Oakes (Eds.), *Early category and concept development: Making sense of the blooming, buzzing confusion* (pp. 213–241). New York, NY: Oxford University Press.

Wellman, H. M. (1990). *The child's theory of mind*. Cambridge, MA: MIT Press.

Werker, J. F., Cohen, L. B., Lloyd, V. L., Casasola, M., & Stager, C. L. (1998). Acquisition of word–object associations by 14-month-old infants. *Developmental Psychology*, **34**, 1289–1309.

Westermann, G., & Mareschal, D. (2004). From parts to wholes: Mechanisms of development in infant visual object processing. *Infancy*, **5**, 131–151.

Woodward, A. L. (1998). Infants selectively encode the goal object of an actor's reach. *Cognition*, **69**, 1–34.

Woodward, A. L. (1999). Infants' ability to distinguish between purposeful and non-purposeful behaviors. *Infant Behavior and Development*, **22**, 145–160.

Woodward, A. L., & Hoyne, K. L. (1999). Infants' learning about words and sounds in relation to objects. *Child Development*, **70**, 65–77.

Woodward, A. L., Sommerville, J. A., & Guajardo, J. J. (2001). How infants make sense of intentional action. In B. Malle, L. Moses & D. Baldwin (Eds.), *Intentions and intentionality: Foundations of social cognition* (pp. 149–169). Cambridge, MA: MIT Press.

Xu, F. (1999). Object individuation and object identity in infancy: The role of spatiotemporal information, object property information, and language. *Acta Psychologica*, **102**, 113–136.

Younger, B. A. (1990). Infants' detection of correlations among feature categories. *Child Development*, **61**, 614–620.

Younger, B. A., & Cohen, L. B. (1986). Developmental change in infants' perception of correlations among attributes. *Child Development*, **57**, 803–815.

Younger, B. A., & Gotlieb, S. (1988). Development of categorization skills: Changes in the nature or structure of infant form categories? *Developmental Psychology*, **24**, 611–619.

Younger, B. A., & Johnson, K. E. (2004). Infants' comprehension of toy replicas as symbols for real objects. *Cognitive Psychology*, **48**, 207–242.

ACKNOWLEDGMENTS

Earlier versions and portions of this monograph were presented in seminars at the Department of Psychology at Carnegie Mellon University. We thank David Plaut and Lisa Oakes who provided useful input in the development of the simulations. We also extend gratitude to Jessica Cicchino, Jaime Derringer, Rachel Wu, and the members of the Infant Cognition Laboratory for help in conducting the experiments and to the participants in our studies.

COMMENTARY

ASSOCIATIONIST LEARNING AS A BASIS OF KNOWLEDGE IN INFANCY

Lisa M. Oakes

In this monograph, Rakison and Lupyan outline a framework, *constrained attentional associative learning* (CAAL), to provide a mechanistic explanation for the emergence of conceptual understanding of animacy in infancy. This framework adds to a growing collection of theoretical perspectives asserting that much—if not all—of infants' conceptual understanding derives from general-purpose learning mechanisms, such as detecting of statistical regularities and forming associations between features of objects in the world (e.g., Quinn & Eimas, 1997; Madole & Oakes, 1999; Oakes & Madole, 2003; Smith, Colunga, & Yoshida, 2003). Like these other approaches, Rakison and Lupyan argue for develop mental continuity and increased opportunities to learn and attend to new features and associations with increases in information processing abilities.

The present framework is an important contribution for several reasons. Rakison and Lupyan attempt to specify exactly *what* is continuous and *how* changing information processing abilities create opportunities to learn new features and correlations. Not surprisingly, the discussion here is somewhat vague. However, this work is an excellent example of movement toward deeper understanding of those mechanisms. Second, Rakison and Lupyan's framework makes an important contribution by attempting to simulate infants' perception or understanding of animacy. This is a particularly daring move because children's understanding of animacy (or their related naïve theory of biology or attribution of mental states to others) has been central to theories of conceptual development that appeal to innate domain-specific mechanisms or high-level top-down conceptual constraints on learning (e.g., Keil, 1992; Legerstee, 2001; Leslie, Friedman, &

111

German, 2004). In addition, increasing evidence of specific neurological structures dedicated to human action, as well as neurodevelopmental disorders that apparently lead to deficits in processing such actions, has bolstered claims that such perception must depend on specialized biological mechanisms (e.g., Saxe, 2006). Rakison and Lupyan's alternative to such accounts will certainly elicit criticisms from proponents of more top-down, domain-specific, nativist accounts, and, as they point out, their framework cannot definitively rule out the contribution of such mechanisms. This framework does demonstrate, however, that innate biologically based, top-down, and/or domain-specific mechanisms are not necessary to recognize the distinction between animates and inanimates, at least under some circumstances.

Finally, frameworks like the one outlined here are important because they illustrate that the distinction between perceptual and conceptual knowledge is fuzzy. The blurring of this distinction has become increasingly widespread in both the developmental (Madole & Oakes, 1999; Oakes & Madole, 2003; Smith, 2003) and adult cognitive (Goldstone & Barsalou, 1998) literatures. Although some vigorously hold that conceptual and perceptual knowledge are distinct—and have distinct developmental trajectories (Mandler, 2004)—recently, many researchers have acknowledged that apparently conceptual knowledge must have foundations in perception, and that often it is impossible to draw a clear line that differentiates conceptual and perceptual knowledge or representations. The current framework adds to this discussion by demonstrating how one domain that has clear conceptual implications—animacy—can be rooted in early perceptual processes. In the following sections these contributions will be discussed.

THE REVIVAL OF ASSOCIATIONIST MECHANISMS OF LEARNING AND DEVELOPMENT

Obviously, associationist accounts of learning and development are not new. However, for many years such accounts often were described as too simplistic or low-level to provide deep insight into high-level cognitive processes and conceptual understanding. As Rakison and Lupyan point out, such accounts historically have been criticized for being too unconstrained, and as a result there is nothing to stop infants and young children from attending to uninformative associations (e.g., mothers are associated with walls) as well as informative ones. Recent demonstrations, however, have shown that such models *can* explain developmental change—even apparently qualitative changes in behavior (see Elman,

Bates, Johnson, Karmiloff-Smith, Parisi, & Plunkett, 1996, for a particularly compelling example). Moreover, it has become clear that learning can occur as a result of domain-general constraints and the structure inherent in the *input*.

Domain-General Constraints

Like many associationist learning frameworks, Rakison and Lupyan assume that the initial constraints of the system are domain-general. Such domain-general constraints can produce apparently domain-specific developmental effects (Elman, 2005). For Rakison and Lupyan's *constrained attentional associationist learning* attention is biased to be directed toward some types of stimuli. For example, moving stimuli are better at capturing attention than are nonmoving stimuli. Such constraints are well supported by the literature: Motion is effective at capturing attention (e.g., Girelli & Luck, 1997) and infants prefer moving stimuli to stationary ones (e.g., Shaddy & Colombo, 2004).

However, despite the effort to characterize the initial constraints, the precise nature of these constraints remains unclear. For example, the constraints are referred to as *inherent*, but it is not clear what distinguishes inherent and innate constraints. In addition, the bases of the constraints are not specified. There are several reasons why the system might be biased to attend to moving stimuli. For example, from birth subcortical structures such as the superior colliculus are functional in controlling visual attention; cortical control of visual attention develops over the first several months (Colombo, 2001). Early biases toward moving visual stimuli over static visual stimuli may reflect this subcortical control—input to the superior colliculus is based heavily on the magnocellular pathway that is sensitive to motion. Biases toward moving stimuli may also reflect movement being specified by transients that are more detectable by the visual system than are non-transient visual events. Rakison and Lupyan do not spell out whether such low-level processes drive the inherent biases in their system—and it seems unlikely that by 20 months such factors would completely explain differences in attention to some features over the others. Perhaps low-level factors constrain visual attention early in development, creating biases that persist into late infancy and toddlerhood.

In addition, Rakison and Lupyan do not specify what is meant by *attention*. There are many varieties of attention (Luck & Vecera, 2002), and presumably different aspects of attention would have different kinds of constraints. It seems unlikely, for example, that the executive aspects of attention would be biased toward moving versus stationary stimuli. Thus, in Rakison and Lupyan's framework low-level visual attention may be constrained, but this is not well specified in the model.

The point is that this framework would benefit from precision in spelling out exactly what is meant by constraints on attention—particularly because this aspect of the framework has the burden of answering criticisms that associationist learning mechanisms are too powerful and unconstrained. Despite these limitations, Rakison and Lupyan's framework advances the field by taking seriously the nature of domain-general constraints, and providing an important starting point for developing hypotheses for understanding how such constraints on the attentional system could influence learning.

Structure of the Input

Also consistent with other associationist models is the contribution of the structure of the input to learning. In many domains, theorists have argued that it would be impossible to extract statistical regularities from the input provided—because the input underdetermines what must be learned (e.g., Lidz & Waxman, 2004; Lidz, Waxman, & Freedman, 2003). These arguments are pervasive despite the fact that researchers and theoreticians have demonstrated that complex cognitive things—such as syntax and word-object referents—*can* be learned from the input (e.g. Seidenberg, 1997; Yu & Smith, 2007). That is, despite the fact that the input is messy, statistical regularities are only probabilistic, and spurious correlations exist, powerful associationist learning systems can extract regularities and learn the input, even without highly constrained domain-specific mechanisms. Simulations like those provided here show that yet another important distinction—indeed, one that can easily be argued to be driven by top-down processes—can be learned from the input.

THE PROBLEM OF ANIMACY

Infants' ability to discriminate animates from inanimates has been the focus of discussions about conceptual development. Indeed, it has been argued that understanding children's developing representation of animacy can shed light on key issues in conceptual development, such as whether there are innate concepts and whether complex concepts can emerge bottom-up from perceptual learning mechanisms (Gelman & Opfer, 2002). Clearly, the present monograph fits squarely in this discussion. An important component of this debate is when infants understand that animate beings engage in goal directed actions. Some researchers have argued that infants have specialized knowledge of the cues that specify intentional agents (Johnson, 2003; Saxe, Tzelnic, & Carey, 2007). The kinds of cues proposed in these models—and how infants develop knowledge of those cues—are quite different from the ones proposed by Rakison and Lupyan. Whereas the current framework proposes that the discrimination of animates and inanimates derives from general-purpose attentional mechanisms, these other models propose that this type of discrimination derives from a sensitivity to ontological kinds (Saxe et al., 2007) or from innate imitation abilities allowing infants to map the behavior of others onto mental states (Meltzoff & Decety, 2003). Thus, these approaches are centered around the notion that infants have some domain-specific biases to attend to some kinds of information or that innate processes allow them to learn about the goal-directedness of human (and animate) action.

Rakison and Lupyan's model makes great strides toward demonstrating that even recognizing the distinction between animates and inanimates can be achieved with general-purpose associationist learning mechanisms. Of course, this is only a demonstration that infants' perception of a small class of events can be explained in this way. Clearly, until the model is tested on a broader set of stimuli it is unknown how effective this learning mechanism will be at explaining infants' discrimination of animates and inaminates (and their perception of goal directed agency) more generally. However, this framework represents and important step in such a demonstration; it shows how at least one class of stimuli can be explained using this general purpose learning mechanisms, illustrating that such mechanisms are sufficient to make these distinctions. It seems plausible—and even likely—that models like these can explain other distinctions infants make that have been attributed to a sophisticated understanding of animacy and goal-directed behavior.

THE ISSUE OF PERCEPTUAL VERSUS CONCEPTUAL PROCESSES

Finally, accounts like that presented here is it makes clear that the distinction between *perception* and *conception* is blurry. Much has been made about the difference between perceptual groupings and perceptual groupings. For example, researchers have designed studies to determine whether children rely more on perceptual (surface features) or perceptual (labels) information by pitting the two kinds of information against one another (e.g., Gelman & Markman, 1987). Others have argued for different processes for grouping objects using perceptual and conceptual information (Mandler, 2004).

However, the distinction between perceptual and conceptual information is not that clear. As we have pointed out, perceptual and conceptual information often seem to lie on a continuum from "low-level" surface feature information (e.g., color) to "higher-level" more abstract features (e.g., has dog DNA) (Madole & Oakes, 1999). Similarly, Goldstone and Barsalou (1998) have argued that even for adults perceptual and conceptual information are not clearly distinct. The present framework shows how *perceptual* information can specify what is (for adults) a *conceptual* distinction. Thus, perspectives like that presented here provide a foundation for arguments that detection of perceptual regularities bootstraps higher-level conceptual understanding. This contrasts with Quinn and Eimas's (1997) proposal that early perceptual distinctions are enriched through the addition of higher-level conceptual information, such as labels. The present account is more sophisticated, and argues that infants detect perceptual regularities and then their recognition of (or attention to) those regularities is constrained by additional knowledge and experience; thus resulting in more than "merely perceptual" groupings, bur rather groupings that are based on "conceptual" theories of the world. In many ways, the current framework demonstrates how thinking about such mechanisms has evolved since Quinn and Eimas's important paper. Rakison and Lupyan's framework is the next generation of these models and illustrates a deeper understanding derived from an additional decade of research for how conceptual understanding can derive from perceptual processes.

Rakison and Lupyan's framework therefore adds to a body of work illustrating the fuzziness of the distinction between perceptual and conceptual knowledge. This is an important addition because although other demonstrations have shown that associationist networks can adequately account for aspects of language development (Smith et al., 2003) and perceptual categorization of images of animals (Mareschal, French, & Quinn, 2000), the present framework is one of a few that shows that such networks can account for infants' apparently *conceptual* processing. Rakison and Lupyan have shown that an associationist network can differentiate animates from inanimates, and causal agents from objects that do not act as causal agents. As described above, infants' understanding of this distinction has been explained in terms of top-down, inferential, domain-specific mechanisms.

Rakison and Lupyan's simulations show how this distinction can be made even by bottom-up, perceptual learning mechanisms. Thus, the simulations reported here provide an critically important demonstration that this distinction can be learned solely through forming perceptual associations, and that such associations might form the foundation and bootstrap later conceptual understanding of those distinctions. Importantly, the mechanism by which these early perceptual associations would develop into deeper conceptual understanding of the distinction is not the type of enrichment described by Quinn and Eimas (1997). Rather, Rakison and

Lupyan propose that deeper conceptual understanding arises from the development of information processing abilities (and knowledge) that allow infants to recognize more subtle and sophisticated associations between dynamic features of objects—including those involving dynamic, transient object labels. In support of this proposal, Rakison and Lupyan simulate the behavior of infants in a habituation experiment in which labels are correlated with other features, and then demonstrate that human infants show the pattern predicted by the simulation. Generating novel predictions and then testing them with infants is an important feature of such frameworks. As a result of this aspect of Rakison and Lupyan's work, the framework they propose will generate hypotheses and provide the foundation of a mechanistic explanation for infants' developing conceptual understanding of animacy.

CONCLUSIONS

In summary, the framework described by Rakison and Lupyan is a viable alternative to approaches that assume that the animate–inanimate distinction can only be made by applying conceptual knowledge top-down. The simulations presented here demonstrate the sufficiency of a bottom-up approach and show how a rich conceptual system can emerge from low-level perceptual input and the detection of statistical regularities. Moreover, the model goes beyond simply describing developmental change and makes a real effort to explain the mechanisms of that change. Only time will tell whether those mechanisms are the right ones; but this theory provides an important starting point for examining such mechanisms in infants' learning about animacy. Thus, this model is innovative and will provide important challenges to future work on the developmental origins of the ability to differentiate animates from inanimates.

References

Colombo, J. (2001). The development of visual attention in infancy. *Annual Review of Psychology*, **52**, 337–367.

Elman, J. L. (2005). Connectionist models of cognitive development: Where next? *Trends in Cognitive Sciences*, **9**, 112–117.

Elman, J. L., Bates, E. A., Johnson, M. H., Karmiloff-Smith, A., Parisi, D., & Plunkett, K. (1996). *Rethinking innateness: A connectionist perspective on development*. Cambridge, MA: MIT Press.

Gelman, S. A., & Markman, E. M. (1987). Young children's inductions from natural kinds: The role of categories and appearances. *Child Development*, **58**, 1532–1541.

Gelman, S. A., & Opfer, J. E. (2002). *Development of the animate–inanimate distinction*. Malden, MA: Blackwell Publishing.

Girelli, M., & Luck, S. J. (1997). Are the same attentional mechanisms used to detect visual search targets defined by color, orientation, and motion? *Journal of Cognitive Neuroscience*, **9**, 238–253.

Goldstone, R. L., & Barsalou, L. W. (1998). Reuniting perception and conception. *Cognition*, **65**, 231–262.

Johnson, S. C. (2003). Detecting agents. *Philosophical Transactions of the Royal Society of London, B*, **358**, 549–559.

Keil, F. C. (1992). The origins of an autonomous biology. In M. R. Gunnar & M. Maratsos (Eds.), *Modularity and constraints in language and cognition: The Minnesota symposia on child psychology* (Vol. 25, pp. 103–137). Hillsdale, NJ: Erlbaum.

Legerstee, M. (2001). Domain specificity and the epistemic triangle: The development of the concept of animacy in infancy. In F. Lacerda, C. von Hofsten, & M. Heimann (Eds.), *Emerging cognitive abilities in early infancy* (pp. 193–212). Mahwah, NJ: Erlbaum.

Leslie, A. M., Friedman, O., & German, T. P. (2004). Core mechanisms in 'theory of mind'. *Trends in Cognitive Sciences*, **8**, 529–533.

Lidz, J., & Waxman, S. (2004). Reaffirming the poverty of the stimulus argument: A reply to the replies. *Cognition*, **93**, 157–165.

Lidz, J., Waxman, S., & Freedman, J. (2003). What infants know about syntax but couldn't have learned: Experimental evidence for syntactic structure at 18 months. *Cognition*, **89**, B65–B73.

Luck, S. J., & Vecera, S. P. (2002). Attention. In H. Pashler & S. Yantis (Eds.), *Steven's handbook of experimental psychology (3rd ed.), Vol. 1: Sensation and perception* (pp. 235–286). Hoboken, NJ: John Wiley & Sons Inc.

Madole, K. L., & Oakes, L. M. (1999). Making sense of infant categorization: Stable processes and changing representations. *Developmental Review*, **19**, 263–296.

Mandler, J. M. (2004). *The foundations of mind: Origins of conceptual thought*. New York: Oxford University Press.

Mareschal, D., French, R. M., & Quinn, P. C. (2000). A connectionist account of asymmetric category learning in early infancy. *Developmental Psychology*, **36**, 635–645.

Meltzoff, A. N., & Decety, J. (2003). What imitation tells us about social cognition: A rapprochement between developmental psychology and cognitive neuroscience? *Philosophical Transactions of the Royal Society of London, B: Biological Sciences*, **358**, 491–500.

Oakes, L. M., & Madole, K. L. (2003). Principles of developmental change in infants' category formation. In D. H. Rakison & L. M. Oakes (Eds.), *Early category and concept development: Making sense of the blooming, buzzing confusion* (pp. 132–158). New York: Oxford University Press.

Quinn, P. C., & Eimas, P. D. (1997). A reexamination of the perceptual-to-conceptual shift in mental representations. *Review of General Psychology*, **1**, 171–187.

Saxe, R. (2006). Uniquely human social cognition. *Current Opinion in Neurobiology. Special Issue: Cognitive Neuroscience*, **16**, 235–239.

Saxe, R., Tzelnic, T., & Carey, S. (2007). Knowing who dunnit: Infants identify the causal agent in an unseen causal interaction. *Developmental Psychology*, **43**, 149–158.

Seidenberg, M. S. (1997). Language acquisition and use: Learning and applying probabilistic constraints. *Science*, **275**, 1599–1603.

Shaddy, D. J., & Colombo, J. (2004). Developmental changes in infant attention to dynamic and static stimuli. *Infancy*, **5**, 355–365.

Smith, L. B. (2003). Learning to recognize objects. *Psychological Science*, **14**, 244–250.

Smith, L. B., Colunga, E., & Yoshida, H. (2003). Making an ontology: Cross-linguistic evidence. In D. H. Rakison & L. M. Oakes (Eds.), *Early category and concept development: Making sense of the blooming, buzzing confusion* (pp. 275–302). New York: Oxford University Press.

Yu, C., & Smith, L. B. (2007). Rapid word learning under uncertainty via cross-situational statistics. *Psychological Science*, **18**, 414–420.

COMMENTARY

ENCOUNTERING CONCEPTS IN CONTEXT

Arlene S. Walker-Andrews

When I was an undergraduate, a group of us once tested the hypothesis that the lexicon was organized like a dictionary i.e., alphabetically. Using reaction times, we demonstrated convincingly that this was unlikely to be the case. But it occurred to me then that psychologists frequently use humankind's most recent technological inventions as models for human thought processes. Others have studied the use of such metaphors in psychology (e.g., Gentner & Grudin, 1985; Leary, 1990), documenting trends in the choice of metaphors. In cognitive psychology, the computer metaphor has dominated, and very recently, connectionism has become popular as a way to model a wide variety of theoretical perspectives, including behaviorist, nativist, and constructivist. The connectionist approach provides researchers "a set of computational and conceptual tools that can be useful for investigating and rendering specific fundamental issues of human development" (O'Loughlin & Karmiloff-Smith, 2003, p. 614).

In the present monograph, Rakison and Lupyan (R&L) have used connectionist modeling to create a compelling case for the efficacy of general mechanisms in the development of object concepts during infancy. They interleave data from empirical studies of infants' concepts for animates and inanimates with the results of simulations of infants' behavior during acquisition of knowledge about objects' motions, their causal role, the onset of motion, and initial pairing of a label and a moving object. The infant studies demonstrate that babies ranging in age from 10 to 22 months progress systematically in their abilities, moving from global, undifferentiated perception to increased specificity. The simulations also show a trend of "increasingly constrained learning" by way of two parallel learning systems, one "quick-learning but fragile, the other slow-learning and more permanent" (R&L, p. 122). This is an important body of work that demonstrates the power of an integrated research program for predicting the development of infants' categorization and generalization about objects in the world, as well as its promise for examining other cognitive advances.

In this Commentary, I will focus on the role of what Rakison and Lupyan call "attentional biases" for infants' perception and cognition, directions for future research in the area of concept formation, and compare Rakison and Lupyan's approach with another domain-general proposal for word learning. I will end with some observations about more nativist accounts of cognitive development brought to mind by the present monograph.

THE PRIMACY OF MOTION IN PERCEPTION

Rakison and Lupyan propose what they term a "constrained attentional associative learning model" (CAAL) that includes features such as inherent perceptual learning biases as well as more general features of the connectionist architecture such as domain-general associative learning and continuous, incremental augmentation of the initial representations. The major attention bias included in the simulations and assumed for human infants is a preference for motion. This preference is termed *inherent* by Rakison and Lupyan. They assert that such preferences are "present at birth or shortly thereafter and that although they require input to be activated, they are not an emergent property of learning . . . [rather they are] evolved adaptations that are part of the human visual system and are shared with other animals" (R&L, p. 27).

I could not agree more with the notion that young infants are especially drawn to motion, and that perceptual learning progresses most rapidly when infants encounter and are involved in events. The bulk of my own research has focused on the importance of dynamic, multimodal expressive events for infants' appreciation of the meaning of emotions. Therefore, I am somewhat puzzled by the distinctions Rakison and Lupyan make about infants' attention to dynamic information and their learning about dynamic properties of animals, vehicles, people, and other animate and inanimate objects. They assert, "Although dynamic information is highly salient, it requires considerable information-processing abilities to track and encode an object's static and dynamic features as they move" (R&L, p. 29). Contrast this to older findings. A series of studies conducted by Gibson and her colleagues (Gibson, Owsley, & Johnston, 1978; Gibson, Owsley, Walker, & Megaw-Nyce, 1979; Walker, Owsley, Megaw-Nyce, Gibson, & Bahrick, 1980) demonstrated that infants as young as 3 months could discriminate and generalize motions characteristic of rigid or elastic objects, as well as abstract information for shape across motion. Results from crossmodal studies contribute to the impression that infants use motion information effectively. For example, Walker-Andrews and Lennon (1985) found that infants as young as 5 months could detect the relation between the sight and sound of a receding or approaching object (see also Pickens, 1994).

So what is it that differentiates infants' performance in a host of studies in which they demonstrate exquisite sensitivity to motion and an ability to discern emotion, shape, substance, distance, and other object and event properties when these are revealed by motion? Rakison and Lupyan discuss a number of similar studies and suggest several possibilities: in many such experiments infants were not required to attend to an object over time and space; dynamic features may attract attention, but may be more difficult to discriminate than static features; or young infants cannot "encode relations among dynamic cues that involve relatively complex information related to motion characteristics of objects and entities (e.g., agency, self-propulsion)" (p. 30). Perhaps the authors are making a distinction between moving parts (calling them dynamic features) and other motions, but the texture elements of an elastic object move in relation to one another when the object is deformed, and, in the case of facial features, move somewhat independently during portrayal of an emotional expression.

Given the importance of motion and context to Rakison and Lupyan's CAAL model, the role of motion, types of motion, and details of stimulus information demand closer inspection. Rakison and Lupyan make headway in some respects, for example, by contrasting motion characteristics of animate and inanimate objects, and by an analysis of the importance to adults of motion-related features in their concepts of animate and inanimate. Nevertheless, the stimulus materials shown to young infants in most of Rakison's empirical research are rigid, geometric figures with surface features and appendages. Infants might respond quite differently if these figures captured other facets typically shown by animate objects, other than hard-bodied insects that scuttle from place to place. Fortunately, the switch procedure that Rakison uses to study infants' concept formation coupled with connectionist modeling is well designed to explore the specific characteristics of motion and the development of responses to it in subsequent studies.

IN PURSUIT OF FURTHER UNDERSTANDING

Rakison and Lupyan recognize that additional work is necessary for a fully fledged theory of concept formation during infancy. They also present five potential criticisms of their framework, including that (a) there are other similar perspectives (e.g., Colunga & Smith, 2002; Eimas & Quinn, 1994; Oakes & Madole, 2003); (b) the data do not refute more nativist views; (c) different neurological structures may support infants' behavior; (d) the model may be too flexible; and (e) connectionist models may be too powerful. Only continued research can provide perspective on these criticisms, and Rakison and Lupyan propose future directions for that purpose. To the list of future studies, I propose some additions, including the use of converging methods (cf. Garner, 1974), testing atypically developing infants and children, and refinements to the simulations in response to findings from such studies.

The use of additional methods to investigate infants' categorization and generalization is obvious. The habituation data produced by experimental and simulation studies indicate that infants will categorize objects such as animals and vehicles first by using surface features involved in motion. According to the present authors, the sequential tracking method (Rakison & Butterworth, 1998; Rakison & Cohen, 1999) and inductive generalization procedure (Rakison, 2005) yield similar results. But will infants also imitate selectively based on observation of specific kinds of motions? That is, will they not only generalize to objects with similar characteristics, but will they generalize types of motion on the same objects, or accompany those imitations with vocalizations and other behaviors that provide converging evidence about their categorization of the objects? Can infants show deferred imitation based on understanding of animacy? Will they apply labels selectively based on similar information? Can researchers test whether objects have different affordances for action based on motion information across a variety of contexts, such as the social referencing paradigm? Although it may be difficult to design, given the power of the intermodal preference technique and variations of habituation procedures that use multimodal information to determine whether infants can detect and learn correspondences, intermodal approaches may also yield important information.

Second, testing children and infants who lag in their demonstration of categorization of objects based on specific types of motion and other properties would be especially useful for identifying parameters to be tested with a connectionist approach. Johnson and Rakison (2006) have reported that children with autism "are delayed in the processes by which they form categories but nonetheless possess relevant knowledge about the motion properties of animates and inanimates" (p. 73). Other groups of children who show delays in categorization or in making distinctions between animate and inanimate objects may well serve as participants. Different methods will be required for these children, both because of their developmental delays, but also because they are more experienced, may have better memories, and possess other cognitive abilities that may not have been similarly affected.

Finally, refinements to the simulations that make use of data from converging methods and atypical populations may lead to further discovery. If indeed children with autism possess knowledge about the motion properties that distinguish animate and inanimate objects, can one develop a model for its development? Can key features of the connectionist model for typically developing children be altered in ways that allow closer inspection of its categorization ability? For example, Bjorne and Balkenius (2005) have published a computational model for attention impairments in children in autism, which focuses on the role of "deficient context processing in autism" (p. 11).

DYNAMIC SYSTEMS APPROACHES

One of the proposals made by Rakison and Lupyan in the present monograph is that the ability to associate two relatively arbitrary dynamic cues can account for early word learning. Similarly, Gogate, Bahrick and I (Gogate, Walker-Andrews, & Bahrick, 2001) argued that the development of word comprehension progresses by way of domain-general processes. We proposed that advances in perceptual and cognitive abilities interact with properties of the environment to influence infants' detection of relationships. Changes in the requisite conditions under which infants learn speech pattern–object relations across experiments demonstrate the dynamic character of infants' developing perceptual–lexical systems. Consistent with a dynamic systems approach, we proposed that infants' word learning reflects "the constant fluctuation in and across parameters . . . . Changes over time may look, on the surface, like regression or U-shaped functions of the co-action of systems and relative weights of parameters" (p. 8).

Despite these points of agreement with Rakison and Lupyan, however, I claim that association is not the appropriate mechanism to invoke for explaining infants' word learning. In my view, infants seek out invariants and patterns in stimulation rather than simply responding wholesale to any co-occurrences. I agree that language-specific mechanisms are not required to account for the ability of infants to detect the arbitrary relations between words and referents, but maintain that association is too passive and that an appeal to that timeworn mechanism does not consider sufficiently the interaction between organism and environment. Gogate et al. pointed out that infants detect intermodal invariants and affordances in the environment, especially as their attention becomes educated, and do not always learn "false" correlations. For example, two decades ago, Bahrick (1988) reported that 3-month-old infants showed intermodal learning based on two types of invariant audio-visual relations, temporal synchrony and temporal microstructure that specified the composition of the object. Intermodal learning did not transpire through association based on co-occurrence, nor did it take place when any incongruent audio-visual structure was present.

In the social-emotional domain, Walker-Andrews and Lennon (1991) studied the process by which infants might come to discriminate vocal expressions by habituating infants to vocal expressions accompanied by an affectively matching facial expression, a facial expression depicting a different emotion, or a checkerboard. On the posttests, 5-month-old infants increased their looking time to any change in vocal expression, except when a checkerboard had been present during the habituation phase. They apparently did not detect a relation between the static, inanimate checkerboard and a vocalization. In the language domain, Kuhl, Williams, & Meltzoff (1991) reported that infants as young as four months did not match two pure tones with the visible mouth shapes of a person articulating the vowels /a/ and /i/. Older infants (7 months) learned an arbitrary relation between /a/ and /i/ and moving objects when those vocalizations coincided with object motions, but not when the sounds were paired with nonmoving objects or when the sounds were presented during pauses between object motions (Gogate & Bahrick, 1998). All of these examples used auditory-visual stimulus materials and the ages of the infants vary from three to seven months, but in each case infants failed to learn inappropriate or incorrect relations.

Rakison and Lupyan acknowledge that "associative learning alone is insufficiently constrained to allow infants to form veridical representations for the objects and entities around them" (R&L, p. 116). Rather than trying to resuscitate the mechanism of association by coupling it with attention biases, Rakison and Lupyan should relegate the term to the dustbin and find or propose a more appropriate descriptive term for the complex, active process that must underlie infants' developing skills at categorizing and generalizing about objects. Rakison and Lupyan do not embed context and real-world constraints in their present account, but enriching the CAAL model with such contextual information is likely to lead to better appreciation of its role in perception and cognition.

OBSERVATIONS ABOUT THE DEVELOPMENT OF WATCHES AND ORGANISMS

A major piece of Rakison and Lupyan's hypothesis is that general mechanisms coupled with maturation of neurological structures and processing abilities suffice to propel the infant from undifferentiated, global perception to acquisition of rudimentary object concepts. They contrast their perspective with that of theorists who propose the existence of specialized mechanisms, modules, or skeletal principles (e.g., Leslie, 1995; Spelke, 1994). Rakison and Lupyan's intriguing description of theoretical differences between these modular approaches and the general mechanism point of view lead to an observation about the similarity in the structure of various approaches. Specifically, for some "the complexity of the input, among other things, implies that concept formation must be supported by specialized, domain-specific mechanisms" (R&L, p. 114). In essence, the more nativist argument appears to be

125

"if it's complicated, general mechanisms won't do." Modern day proponents of "intelligent design" attempt to discard general processes such as natural selection with the claim that an organism's complexity is evidence of a cosmic designer. Those who assert that human mental capacities are domain-specific adaptations specialized with dealing with particular kinds of perceptual cues, conceptual knowledge, and behaviors take a similar tact. At first blush, the contention that two disparate models are similar in structure seems implausible. After all, Cosmides and Tooby (online primer) devised evolutionary psychology as a way to think about how the mind was designed by natural selection to solve adaptive problems, in contrast to what they call the "Standard Social Science Model" (p. 3), which proposes internal general processes, and in contrast to Intelligent Design, which proposes a Prescient Being. However, an examination of the proposed mechanisms for change employed by Evolutionary Psychology and by Intelligent Design models reveals their parallel structures. On paper, Evolutionary Psychology would show natural selection (a general-purpose mechanism) creating a multiplicity of modules in the head to deal with a multiplicity of information sources in the world. Similarly, Intelligent Design would show a box labeled Prescient Being who creates a complex organism to get around in a complex world. A general-purpose mechanism such as association deals directly with the complicated world in a continuous and incremental fashion, without the necessity of a set of intervening structures.

CONCLUSIONS

Rakison and Lupyan have presented a persuasive case for how infants might acquire object concepts and categories, specifically for animate and inanimate objects. They propose that a general-purpose mechanism, association, coupled with constraints on learning such as immature information processing skills and with contextual information may lead to advances in concept formation. They provide simulations of these processes, which fit well with the infant data. The monograph makes a strong contribution to the literature on infants' concept learning. An elaboration that includes encounters with contextual information would provide additional power to the model.

References

Bahrick, L. E. (1988). Intermodal learning in infancy: Learning on the basis of two kinds of invariant relations in audible and visible events. *Child Development*, **59**, 197–209.
Bjorne, P., & Balkenius, C. (2005). A model of attentional impairments in autism: First steps toward a computational theory. *Cognitive Systems Research*, **6**, 193–204.

Colunga, E., & Smith, L. B. (2002). What makes a word? In *Proceedings of the Annual Conference of the Cognitive Science Society, 24* (pp. 214–219). Mahwah, NJ: Erlbaum.

Cosmides, L., & Tooby, J. (2008). *Evolutionary psychology: A primer.* Retrieved January 2, 2008, from http://www.psych.ucsb.edu/research/cep/primer.html

Eimas, P. D., & Quinn, P. C. (1994). Studies on the formation of perceptually based basic-level categories in young infants. *Child Development, 65,* 903–917.

Garner, W. R. (1974). *The processing of information and structure.* New York: Wiley.

Gentner, D., & Grudin, J. (1985). The evolution of mental metaphors in psychology: A 90-year retrospective. *American Psychologist, 40,* 181–192.

Gibson, E. J., Owsley, C. J., & Johnston, J. (1978). Perception of invariants by five-month-old infants: Differentiation of two types of motion. *Developmental Psychology, 14,* 407–415.

Gibson, E. J., Owsley, C. J., Walker, A. S., & Megaw-Nyce, J. (1979). Development of the perception of invariants: Substance and shape. *Perception, 8,* 609–619.

Gogate, L. J., & Bahrick, L. E. (1998). Intersensory redundancy facilitates learning of arbitrary relations between vowel-sounds and objects in 7-month-olds. *Journal of Experimental Child Psychology, 69,* 133–149.

Gogate, L., Walker-Andrews, A. S., & Bahrick, L. E. (2001). The intersensory origins of word comprehension: An ecological-dynamic systems view. *Developmental Science, 4,* 1–18.

Johnson, C. R., & Rakison, D. (2006). Early categorization of animate/inanimate concepts in young children with autism. *Journal of Developmental and Physical Disabilities, 18,* 73–89.

Kuhl, P. K., Williams, K. A., & Meltzoff, A. N. (1991). Cross-modal speech perception in adults and infants using non-speech auditory stimuli. *Journal of Experimental Psychology: Human Perception and Performance, 17,* 829–840.

Leary, D. E. (Ed.) (1990). *Psyche's muse: The metaphors in the history of psychology.* In D. E. Leary (Ed.), *Metaphor in the history of psychology* (pp. 1–78). New York: Cambridge University Press.

Leslie, A. (1995). A theory of agency. In D. Sperber, D. Premack & A. J. Premack (Eds.), *Causal cognition* (pp. 121–141). Oxford: Clarendon.

Oakes, L. M., & Madole, K. L. (2003). Principles of developmental change in infants; category formation. In D. H. Rakison & L. M. Oakes (Eds.), *Early category and concept development: Making sense of the blooming, buzzing confusion* (pp. 159–172). New York: Oxford University Press.

O'Loughlin, C. F., & Karmiloff-Smith, A. (2003). Evaluating connectionism: A developmental perspective. Commentary on Anderson & Lebierre. *Behavioural and Brain Sciences, 26,* 614–615.

Pickens, J. N. (1994). Perception of auditory-visual distance relations by 5-month-old infants. *Developmental Psychology, 30,* 537–544.

Rakison, D. H. (2005). Developing knowledge of motion properties in infancy. *Cognition, 96,* 183–214.

Rakison, D. H., & Butterworth, G. (1998). Infants' use of parts in early categorization. *Developmental Psychology, 34,* 49–62.

Rakison, D. H., & Cohen, L. B. (1999). Infants' use of functional parts in basic-like categorization. *Developmental Sciences, 2,* 423–432.

Spelke, E. S. (1994). Initial knowledge: Six suggestions. *Cognition, 50,* 431–445.

Walker, A. S., Gibson, E. J., Owsley, C. J., Megaw-Nyce, J., & Bahrick, L. (1980). Detection of elasticity as an invariant property of objects by young infants. *Perception, 9,* 713–718.

Walker-Andrews, A. S., & Lennon, E. M. (1985). Auditory-visual perception of changing distance by human infants. *Child Development, 56,* 544–548.

Walker-Andrews, A. S., & Lennon, E. (1991). Infants' discrimination of vocal expressions: Contributions of auditory and visual information. *Infant Behavior and Development, 14,* 131–142.

CONTRIBUTORS

David H. Rakison (D.Phil., University of Sussex, 1997) is an Associate Professor of Psychology at the Carnegie Mellon University. His research has focused on the development of categorization and induction in the first years of life. In particular, he has studied when and how infants form representations for the various properties of animates and inanimates in the world. He has edited two books on early category and concept development.

Gary Lupyan is a graduate student in the Department of Psychology at Carnegie Mellon University and the Center for the Neural Basis of Cognition. His main interest is in the effects of language on categorization, memory, and attention.

Lisa M. Oakes is a Professor of Psychology and Research Professor at the Center for Mind and Brain at the University of California, Davis. She received her Ph.D. at the University of Texas at Austin. Her research is aimed at understanding how infants attend to, perceive, and represent visually presented objects. She has examined the processes of infants' visual short-term memory, categorization, and selective attention.

Arlene S. Walker-Andrews is currently Associate Provost and Professor of Psychology at the University of Montana. She received her Ph.D. in Psychology at Cornell University in 1980. Her research concerns perceptual and cognitive development, particularly the development of the perception of emotions, intermodal perception during infancy, and young children's understanding of pretense.

STATEMENT OF EDITORIAL POLICY

The *Monographs* series aims to publish major reports of developmental research that generate authoritative new findings and uses these to foster a fresh perspective or integration of findings on some conceptually significant issue. Submissions from programmatic research projects are welcomed; these may consist of individually or group-authored reports of findings from a single large-scale investigation or from a sequence of experiments centering on a particular question. Multiauthored sets of independent studies that center on the same underlying question may also be appropriate; a critical requirement in such instances is that the various authors address common issues and that the contribution arising from the set as a whole be unique, substantial, and well-integrated. Manuscripts reporting interdisciplinary or multidisciplinary research on significant developmental questions and those including evidence from diverse cultural, racial, ethnic, national, or other contexts are of particular interest. Because the aim of the series is not only to advance knowledge on specialized topics but also to enhance cross-fertilization among disciplines or subfields, the links between the specific issues under study and larger questions relating to developmental processes should emerge clearly for both general readers and specialists on the topic. In short, irrespective of how it may be framed, work that contributes significant data or extends developmental thinking will be considered.

Potential authors are not required to be members of the Society for Research in Child Development or affiliated with the academic discipline of psychology to submit a manuscript for consideration by the *Monographs*. The significance of the work in extending developmental theory and in contributing new empirical information is the crucial consideration.

Submissions should contain a minimum of 80 manuscript pages (including tables and references). The upper boundary of 150–175 pages is more flexible, but authors should try to keep within this limit. Please submit manuscripts electronically to the SRCD Monographs Online Submissions and Review Site (MONOSubmit) at www.srcd.org/monosubmit. Please contact the Monographs office with any questions at monographs@srcd.org.

The corresponding author for any manuscript must, in the submission letter, warrant that all coauthors are in agreement with the content of the manuscript. The corresponding author also is responsible for informing all coauthors, in a timely manner, of manuscript submission, editorial decisions, reviews received, and any revisions recommended. Before publication, the corresponding author must warrant in the submissions letter that the study was conducted according to the ethical guidelines of the Society for Research in Child Development.

Potential authors who may be unsure whether the manuscript they are planning would make an appropriate submission are invited to draft an outline of what they propose and send it to the editor for assessment. This mechanism, as well as a more detailed description of all editorial policies, evaluation processes, and format requirements, is given in the "Guidelines for the Preparation of Publication Submissions," which can be found at the SRCD website by clicking on *Monographs*, or by contacting the editor, W. Andrew Collins, Institute of Child Development, University of Minnesota, 51 E. River Road, Minneapolis, MN 55455-0345; e-mail: wcollins@umn.edu.

CURRENT